Retire Wealthy

The Tools You Need to Help Build Lasting Wealth - On Your Own or With Your Financial Advisor

Eric D. Brotman, CFP®

authorHOUSE®

AuthorHouse™ LLC
1663 Liberty Drive
Bloomington, IN 47403
www.authorhouse.com
Phone: 1-800-839-8640

Published by AuthorHouse   06/23/2014

ISBN: 978-1-4969-1124-7 (sc)
ISBN: 978-1-4969-1123-0 (hc)
ISBN: 978-1-4969-1125-4 (e)

Library of Congress Control Number: 2014909146

Contents

For Brooke

The light in my sky

"When anyone has enough money not to work, it's usually because he does."

—Malcolm Forbes

(Republished in *Forbes Magazine*, March 25, 2013)

AUTHOR'S BACKGROUND

Eric D. Brotman, CFP®, AEP®, MSFS is President and Managing Principal of Brotman Financial Group, Inc., an independent firm assisting clients with wealth creation, preservation, and distribution. Mr. Brotman began his financial planning practice in Baltimore in 1994, and founded Brotman Financial Group in 2003.

Mr. Brotman holds a Bachelor of Arts degree from the University of Pennsylvania. He earned his CERTIFIED FINANCIAL PLANNER™ (CFP®) certification in 1998, and completed his Master's Degree in Financial Services (MSFS) at the American College in 2003. He is also a Chartered Life Underwriter (CLU), a Chartered Financial Consultant (ChFC), an Accredited Estate Planner (AEP®), and a Chartered Advisor in Senior Living (CASL). Mr. Brotman is a Registered Representative and Investment Advisor Representative with NFP Securities, Inc.

Mr. Brotman is the author of *"Debt-Free for Life: The Tools You Need to Free Yourself from Debt,"* published in 2009 by One Hour or Less Publishing, LLC. He is a 2006 alumnus of Leadership-Baltimore County and a 2009 alumnus of Leadership Maryland, where he is presently serving as Vice Chairman on the Board of Directors. Mr. Brotman serves on the Board of Trustees and is the chairman of the University Advancement Committee at Stevenson University, where he previously served as an adjunct faculty member, teaching financial planning and investment planning courses to CFP® students. His industry involvement includes being a Past-President and Chairman of the Board of the Financial Planning Association of Maryland.

Mr. Brotman appears regularly on NBC's WBAL TV-11 in Baltimore, and has appeared in *Wall Street Journal, The Baltimore Sun, Baltimore Business Journal, The Daily Record, SmartCEO, Investment Advisor, Fidelity Investor's Weekly, Investment News, Journal of Financial Planning, Wealth Manager,* and numerous other publications. He was recognized as one of the "Maryland Power Players" by *The Gazette of Politics and Business* in 2010 and was named one of the "Very Important Professionals" by *The Maryland Daily Record* in 2011.

AUTHOR'S PURPOSE

Through my nearly 20 years in the financial industry, I am still amazed to find how little most Americans understand about personal finance. This book aims:

1) To provide a financial literacy tool for you to learn the basics.

2) To motivate you to get on the path to financial independence and to have the tools you need to help make the journey a rewarding one.

3) To provide a process and various strategies you can use in doing financial planning and wealth-building on your own or with your financial advisor.

We will begin with some brief philosophy on money, retirement, and wealth creation, followed by questions to help you interview prospective financial advisors to help you on this journey.

We will then discuss the process of data gathering and analysis, detailing the steps to take, pitfalls to avoid, and the desired outcomes of financial planning.

Then we'll address risk management, estate planning, and the building blocks of portfolio creation, before summarizing the ten steps to wealth building and providing some action steps so you can get started.

A word of caution: This book is deliberately written in the first-person tense. References to "I" or "me" are specific to the author. References to "we," "us," "our firm," etc . . . are specific to the author's firm, Brotman Financial Group, Inc. All of these references are being used interchangeably in this volume for readability and convenience.

To the extent possible, I have omitted phrases like "In my opinion," and "In my mind," in the hopes of making the book readable and enjoyable instead of sounding like legalese. Note that unless otherwise attributable to someone in specific cases, everything in this book represents my opinion and should not be used for implementation without proper professional analysis.

This book is not designed to render specific investment or planning advice. Please do not implement any of the suggestions in this book without obtaining appropriate legal, tax, and financial advice from qualified professionals who know enough about you and your personal finances to render appropriate advice for you.

There are several instances in the book when I advocate getting professional advice because financial advisors have training to help see many vantage points that sometimes are hard to see when doing planning on your own. Even the most financially savvy individuals can benefit from some dispassionate advice, in the same way that a world-class athlete still has a coach.

In the end, I hope that the strategies in this book can assist you in charting your course towards financial independence. Here's to a bright financial future!

Sincerely,
Eric D. Brotman, CFP®

CHAPTER ONE

GETTING STARTED

THE BASIC DEFINITIONS UNDERLYING RETIREMENT PLANNING AND WEALTH CREATION

Money is one of the most sought-after and misunderstood concepts in our lives. While most people understand the intrinsic value of money and what it can buy, its many forms can be difficult to grasp, as can strategies for its use and deployment.

The concept of "money" is frequently confused with "currency," that is, the paper or coins that stand for various monetary values. If we asked people around the world to show us an example of "money," in most instances they would pull local currency out of their pockets or purses as a demonstration.

In truth, money is much more encompassing, and we'll examine how that is so.

We also need to define ambiguous terms like "financial planning," "retirement," and "wealth" in our analysis, as there are as many definitions of those terms as there are people defining them.

Let's begin our conversation with a few brief definitions:

MONEY: Wikipedia defines money as "any object or record that is generally accepted as payment for goods and services and repayment of debts." In practice, that could include items of exchange or barter, either tangible or intangible, as well as items with intrinsic value like precious metals, or what is otherwise a worthless piece of paper or non-precious metal in your pocket, but for the fact that everyone agrees to a value based on the numbers printed on it.

Some forms of money are readily accessible, and some are not. Some are generally acceptable forms of payment in various geographic areas, while others are not. For example, if I went to get an oil change in my car and in lieu of a few dollars I offered my mechanic some livestock (presumably worth at least as many dollars as the oil change itself), my mechanic would not be likely to accept that form of payment and would likely refuse to change the oil for me.

That unlikely example highlights the need to agree on a definition of "money" for the balance of this book. For our purposes, money will encompass any item of financial value—including intangible financial assets like bank accounts, insurance policies, mutual funds, stocks and bonds, and tangible assets like collectibles, artwork, automobiles, gold, etc.

FINANCIAL PLANNING: Throughout the book, the term "financial planning," will include the decision-making process around all assets, as well as cash management and budgeting, debt management, risk management and insurance, portfolio design, asset allocation, and estate planning. It will also encompass the qualitative decision-making processes around such things as employment, healthcare, family matters, and end-of-life planning, for example.

RETIREMENT: The term "retirement" strikes me as a bit of a misnomer. That is because the root of the word is "retire," and to retire is to "withdraw" or "retreat." I can't imagine why anyone would sign up for that!

The famous football coach from Florida State University, Bobby Bowden, who coached into his 80s, was once asked when he was going to retire, and he said, "I guess I'll retire someday if I live that long." He said that retirement was the next-to-last milestone in his life and that he wasn't ready to have his *last* milestone next up on his list!

The concept of retirement has been around for centuries. The idea was that people would work for their entire adult lives, until one day they either couldn't do the job anymore physically, or some other reason forced them to leave their employment. Within a short period of time, they were deceased. Sound like fun?

In the U.S., "retirement age" is often set as a somewhat arbitrary figure imposed by an employer or the government, like the age at which one becomes eligible for a pension or Social Security Income.

However, when Social Security was created, most people joined the workforce by 18 years of age, worked until they were 65, and were dead by 72. Today, many people don't join the workforce until after college or graduate school (say 22 to 25), they want to retire at 55, and could live to be 107. Needless to say, the old model won't work in most cases.

Some people think of retirement today as working one job instead of two, while others think of it as time on their yacht in the Mediterranean. Clearly, they can't use the same definition or measuring instrument to determine what retirement is or is not.

For our purposes, let's use the following to define "retirement"—the age or moment in life when work becomes *optional*. That way, for those who want to start businesses after leaving the employ of another, or for those who want to get the gold watch and ride off into the sunset, everyone is covered by the same standard. When you have achieved enough financial wherewithal to eschew any and all income-producing activities other than those you *want* to pursue, in my mind you are "retired." **In other words, it is the absence of *needing to work*, not the absence of *working* that defines retirement.**

While we're at it, I would propose that we all think of "retirement" more along the lines of "graduation." A graduation is always something to celebrate—a new chapter, opportunity, or series of life choices. It is a new door being opened. Since retirement sounds like a door being closed, I prefer to think of the positive versus the negative and would rather experience the excitement of launching "Eric Brotman 2.0" when I retire, as opposed to withdrawing and retreating from life.

WEALTH: I am often amused at the media's constant misuse of the term "wealth." How many times have you read that one county or one state is the wealthiest in the country, only to find that what they mean is that the median household income in those areas is the highest? Let me be absolutely clear on this . . . **income does not equal wealth.**

Income is nothing more than an accounting concept for the top line in a personal financial statement. It is a factor in wealth building, but it is not the defining factor.

Wealth is a quantitative measure of prosperity. It is also a qualitative concept, the idea that one "has wealth" or is a "wealthy individual." But wealth is also incredibly relative. As a friend paraphrases from a Bulgarian proverb, "to be wealthy is to be doing better than your neighbor."

Illustrated another way, comedian Chris Rock once quipped about wealth by saying that if Bill Gates woke up tomorrow with Oprah Winfrey's net worth, he would feel poor and want to jump out a window! On the other hand, I would manage to "get by" on Oprah's net worth, thank you.

Since everyone has a relative measure of wealth, for the purpose of this book, let's define wealth as

having achieved financial independence through obtaining enough assets to render earning income unnecessary for the rest of one's life.

Of course there are several paths to immediate wealth—inheritance, the lottery, being a number one pick in the NFL draft, etc. But, since most of us will not inherit life-altering money from Great Aunt Sally, will not hit the Powerball™ jackpot, and will not play quarterback for the Dallas Cowboys, let's concentrate instead on how the rest of us can get there.

Thus, for our purposes, **we are going to look to building wealth gradually, through making a series of financial decisions and crafting a plan to reach a level of prosperity that makes work optional.** I will share some personal stories and examples along the way, along with insights to assist you in setting your vision and following-through on your course.

Let's start by discussing the process of financial planning.

CHAPTER TWO

PROCESS OVERVIEW

THE SIX STEPS TO CREATING A FINANCIAL PLAN

Financial planning requires a series of steps that must be undertaken in sequence to be effective. As with any great recipe, adding ingredients or taking action out of order can adversely impact the outcome of a meal.

Certified Financial Planner™ Practitioners abide by a six-step process for financial planning as established by the CFP® Board of Standards. Those six steps are as follows:

1) Establishing and defining the client-planner relationship.
2) Gathering client data, including goals.
3) Analyzing and evaluating your financial status.
4) Developing and presenting financial planning recommendations and/or alternatives.
5) Implementing the financial planning recommendations.
6) Monitoring the financial planning recommendations.

We will explore each of these steps in greater detail below.

1) Establishing and defining the client-planner relationship.

If you are electing to utilize the services of a financial professional, or considering doing so, it is important to establish and define the relationship first. To do so requires agreeing on several key points:

- **What services does the advisor provide personally?**

In other words, you want to know if the advisor provides recommendations on all of the services in a comprehensive plan, or only on a few services. If the advisor is a stock broker, for example, he or she might limit the scope of your relationship together to just your investment or retirement portfolio. In most cases, you'll want to work with someone who can bring your entire plan into focus and can aid in the execution of that plan.

- **What are the fees and costs of doing business with this advisor?**

There are several ways in which advisors are compensated, and they are regulated by the types of licenses held by the advisor, not by his or her professional designations. Only registered representatives or investment advisory representatives can earn fees for investment advice or commissions on financial products.

Advisors can be paid in a number of different ways:

- By a flat project or engagement fee
- By an hourly or other time-based fee
- By an annual (or periodic) retainer fee
- By a fee expressed as a percentage of assets under management
- By commissions for making transactions

If you are paying fees for planning services, generally you need to know if there are fees associated with each meeting or conversation, or if the services are bundled.

While none of these compensation arrangements is "good" or "bad" per se, I believe that the best way to get comprehensive advice is on a fee-basis or based on a percentage of assets under management. That way, a client pays an advisor to perform analysis and provide recommendations that are not tied solely to the sale of one or more products.

- **How often will the advisor meet with you?**

This is really a personal preference question and is often a function of the complexity of your personal finances. However you want to establish this up-front so that you aren't surprised six months into the engagement.

I know some investment firms that hold portfolio reviews as frequently as once per quarter, while others only meet with their clients on an "as requested" basis. I believe that the ideal meeting schedule is one full annual review meeting, along with a year-end planning call for tactical and/or tax decisions that need to be made by December 31st. An advisor and his or her team should also be available throughout the year when challenges or opportunities arise.

- **How much communication can you expect on an ongoing basis?**

In addition to personal meetings or telephone calls, what other communication can you expect from your advisor? Some advisory firms limit their correspondence to monthly or quarterly statements, while others mail out quarterly newsletters or performance reports, or send periodic e-mails with market news or planning ideas. Some host seminars for the public, while others limit their speaking engagements to private client-only affairs.

Ideally, an advisor should try to communicate frequently without being overwhelming, perhaps with a brief weekly e-mail and monthly electronic reports in addition to basic statements and confirmations. For any planning firm, it is a delicate balance, and one that is ever-changing based on the make-up of the firm's clientele.

- **Does your advisor have other team members who are available to you?**

Knowing the size and depth of your advisor's team will be critically important to you, especially if you value frequent communication with your advisory firm. In some firms, a single assistant may be servicing the clients of six or more advisors, while in other firms there may be a team of licensed professionals ready to assist with your planning.

If your advisor shares an assistant, you are likely with an organization that only handles some small portion of the financial planning process.

I believe that the ideal ratio is two assistants or staff members for each advisor, to make sure that there is depth at every position. Thus, if an advisor is out of the office, clients can continue to interact with the team and get the vast majority of questions answered or needs met.

- **Who are the typical clients of this advisor or firm?**

It is important to have a sense of who the advisor's other clients are to make sure you are a good fit. You'll want to know if you'll be an advisor's biggest client—or smallest one. You may also want to know, for example, if you'll be a 34-year old client at a firm specializing in planning for retirees.

In our firm, we work with multi-generational families, initially engaging with clients who are 45-60 years old and who have to worry simultaneously about caring for aging parents, educating children or grandchildren, and planning for their own retirement. We often work with our clients' parents and children and provide a full spectrum of multi-generational services. Other firms have their own niche clientele, and ideally you want to find a firm specializing in clients who are a lot like you!

- **What is the advisor's planning and investment philosophy?**

In an ideal situation, you want your advisor's philosophy and yours to be in harmony. For example, if you are risk averse, you may not want to work with an advisor promoting his or her short-term stock-picking success. Does your advisor believe in a buy-and-hold strategy with passive management, or does he or she try to time markets or make frequent tactical changes, and how does that correspond with your objectives? Does the advisor favor a more offensive or defensive posture to planning?

All of these questions will help you determine if the potential advisor is a good fit for you and your family on a personal level. These questions will not determine if the advisor is good or bad at what he or she does. Again, it is about specifically matching your preferences and personality with an advisor's.

- **Does the planner represent specific companies or products?**

It can be difficult to know if you are getting objective advice when an advisor's compensation is driven by product sales. Whether the advisor's recommendation is to buy a mutual fund, an annuity, or an insurance product or even to hire a proprietary money manager, it is a potential conflict of interest upon which you should request disclosure in advance of engaging in the planning relationship.

At the end of the day, in making a decision about who to hire to help you manage your finances, I believe you should do everything in your power to make certain that your advisor is representing your best interests at all times.

The up-front disclosure of potential conflicts of interests does not preclude objectivity in rendering advice. However, if the advice you receive is heavily or entirely reliant on proprietary products, you may want to seek a second opinion prior to engaging.

- **How does the advisor select specialists?**

Because the financial planning process will often involve a team of specialists (for more on building your own personal "Dream Team," see Chapter Eight), you need to know how your potential advisor chooses specialists to work with you, and to know if he or she is willing to work with your existing specialists.

These specialists may include: accountants, attorneys, financial institutions (like banks or credit unions), insurance agents, real estate agents, mortgage brokers, money managers, and others.

Think of your financial advisor as your general contractor and the specialists as the sub-contractors. The outcome of your work with this advisor can often rely on the quality of the specialists they or you choose.

Ideally, you want an advisor who will work with your existing specialists, or who can make referrals to ancillary professionals who are considered experts in their fields, and who will not be reliant solely on in-house specialists or staff. You should <u>never</u> be required to use any specific specialist to maintain a relationship with your financial advisor.

- **Will you have online access to your planning and accounts?**

This is increasingly becoming a moot point, only because having online access to accounts is not as much an "option" as it is a basic necessity in today's world. However, it is worth asking what type of access is available, what systems maintain the data, and what security measures are in place to protect the online data. You may also want to ask if the data generation and storage is completed in-house, or by a third-party vendor.

In our firm we use a third-party vendor for online access for several reasons. First, it allows us to focus on financial planning instead of being an IT firm. Second, it allows our clients to know that an independent third-party custodian is maintaining the integrity of the data. While we know the integrity we bring to the table in our dealings with the public, for clients (especially new clients of any firm or advisor) it is nice to, as Ronald Reagan once quipped, "Trust, but verify."

- **Does the advisor have plans to grow the firm and how might that impact your relationship moving forward?**

This is a very important point and one that is frequently overlooked. If your advisor builds a solo practice to the point that he or she can no longer service clients effectively, communication breakdowns are possible. In addition, you may not want to be "handed off" to another advisor in a firm if it effectively ends the relationship you had with your own trusted advisor.

The future of the financial advisory business is captured in the term "ensemble practice." That term has generated volumes of professional articles and books, but it is generally accepted to mean a firm with clients who are serviced by multiple advisors, rather than having a relationship exclusively with one advisor.

Working with an ensemble practice benefits clients, as it provides depth of knowledge, continuity and convenience of advice, collaborative professional advice generation, and a deeper relationship with a team of people. It also benefits advisors, who can leverage one another's strengths and can create professional synergies that a solo practice cannot replicate.

- **Lastly, and perhaps most importantly, does the planner utilize a commercial custodian or other entity to safeguard client assets**?

The safeguarding of client assets is something that should be a given with any financial firm. However, in the wake of various scandals (see also: Bernie Madoff) the security and validity of client accounts is being called into question like never before.

Most financial firms employ a clearing firm to handle the safeguarding and segregation of client assets, and to take them out of the hands of the advisors themselves. Essentially, it provides a client with the comfort of third-party oversight for the custody of their assets. There are a number of large clearing firms in the U.S., with the most notable being National Financial Services (NFS, LLC), Pershing, and Charles Schwab.

Note that some very large firms are "self-clearing" which means that they are the custodians for their own client assets. As long as these are legitimate firms, it is neither a "good" or "bad" arrangement, it is just a way of doing business. Either way, you should *never* be asked to write a check directly to your advisor, nor should your advisor ever accept cash from you. Your advisor and advisory firm have legal responsibilities not to co-mingle assets amongst multiple clients, and not to lend money to or to borrow money from a client. There is a laundry-list of other restricted activities, any of which should raise a red flag for consumers. For more information, you can check out the regulatory websites for FINRA or the SEC.

The responses to these types of questions will help define what you are personally seeking from the advisor, so you can determine how you want to proceed and can evaluate the responses based on your needs. An advisor's response to these questions will help you determine if the potential advisor is a good fit for you and your family on a personal level. Note that these questions will not determine if the advisor is good or bad at what he or she does; again it is about specifically matching your preferences and personality with an advisor's.

*   *   *   *   *

We have talked at length about what you should expect from your advisor in establishing and defining the relationship, but what about what the advisor might expect <u>from you</u>? Let's discuss some of the items that you want to explore to determine what your role in the engagement might be:

- In most cases, to do an excellent job of financial planning, an advisor will expect you to be forthright with your financial picture, and open to discussions about sensitive issues, like family medical history, interpersonal family relationships, and so forth.

- If you are married or in a committed relationship, it is generally important to have both individuals at each meeting, so that everyone is on the same page. I have seen many financial planning conversations turn in dramatically different directions when both partners are asked the same question and give different answers. For example, I remember asking one couple how long they planned to stay in their present home. The husband said, "Indefinitely" and the wife said, "About 12 months." They just looked at each other dumbfounded at how they had no idea the way the other felt on the subject. I turned to the husband and delicately advised him to get some boxes ready for the big move!

- It may also be necessary for you to gather documents, contact former employers, make changes to employee benefits, or take other steps to make the plan accurate or up to date. Oftentimes, clients find the up-front work to be a bit onerous, but once the planning process has been implemented, most of the ongoing work falls squarely on the advisors' shoulders and not on the clients'.

This concludes the section on establishing and defining the client-planner relationship. Let's move forward with step two of the financial planning process . . .

*   *   *   *   *

2) Gathering client data, including goals.

Think of the financial planning process like a physical exam at your doctor's office. Before any diagnoses, treatments, or prognoses are possible, a full head-to-toe examination is required. In addition, your doctor will need to know about family history, health history, lifestyle choices and habits, etc . . . to complement the results of various medical tests.

The financial planning process is just as intimate and involved as the physical exam, and while it never requires wearing an uncomfortable and ill-fitting hospital gown, it does involve discussions on matters well beyond the scope of "money issues."

The data gathering process begins with a questionnaire to allow for self-reporting of various accounts and to take a first shot at financial and non-financial life goals. This questionnaire is usually accompanied by a document checklist—literally a laundry list of documents and other items to bring to your initial planning meeting. These items will allow you and/or your planner to begin to take inventory and to determine where you are in your wealth building odyssey. We will address this inventory process at length in Chapter Three.

A typical questionnaire can vary from a one or two page summary to a much longer and more thorough document. A sample questionnaire is provided in Appendix A. It is 13 pages in length and is designed to capture all of the quantitative client data in one location. A questionnaire like this allows an advisor to spend time with his or her clients discussing the various qualitative issues that directly impact the planning process. These qualitative issues are frequently more important to the outcomes than just the numbers.

Your planner will use your completed questionnaire as the starting point for your discussions together, and will often ask dozens of follow-up questions to verify information and clarify intentions. It allows the *why* and the *how* questions to be answered, as the questionnaire can only adequately capture the *who*, *what*, *where*, and *when* related to your financial world.

Topics frequently covered by an initial questionnaire include: family data, assets and liabilities, employee benefits and insurance coverage, and a basic risk tolerance exercise to begin assessing your comfort level with the investment world.

You will find that the sample questionnaire is very thorough and asks for a lot of information. However, in most cases, several sections (and even several pages) may be entirely blank. We find that it is better to ask for more information than is likely to exist, rather than asking for too little and missing a key element to a family's plan.

The document checklist requests information related to taxes, legal documents, real estate, insurance, employee benefits, bank and investment accounts, debt statements, and personal property, as well as providing a space for other items relevant to your specific situation.

For business owners, there may be a separate and distinct checklist for items related to your enterprise, if you are engaging with a planner for business planning, in addition to family financial planning.

A sample document checklist for personal financial planning can be found in Appendix B.

Between the financial questionnaire and document checklist, you can see that a lot of work is initially required on a client's part. You will find that by working with a team of advisors you will outsource much of the work that follows financial plan implementation. However, if you elect to do some or all of the work on your own the following steps will provide a guide for getting you started.

*   *   *   *   *

3) Analyzing and evaluating your financial status.

Once you have gathered all of the relevant information in one place, it is time to begin synthesizing that information into something organized and digestible. Some financial planning software will allow you to do this on your own, often helping to prepare budgets, savings goals, and tax preparation. One program I particularly like for home use is Quicken™ by Intuit. Quicken™ is readily available, downloads data directly from banks and financial institutions, and is reasonably priced (under $100).

Many financial advisors will use more sophisticated planning software to create various types of models on your behalf. However, in my experience, I find that paying a financial advisory firm to crunch these numbers into a computer and to generate a 100-page report often filled with stock language and diagrams is a waste of time, energy, and money. The problem with these plans is that they are static. That is, they are a snapshot in time and require lots of additional work to modify them later as your life changes. I also find that these reports sit on a shelf, collecting dust, and that the recommendations in them often do not get implemented.

Imagine going to a nutritionist, dietician, or personal trainer to try to get healthy and being presented with a thick three-ring binder of recommendations. You could more easily digest a simple summary of action steps and a brief synopsis, making the suggestions easier to follow.

Financial planning should be approached in the same way. Don't spend thousands of dollars to receive a nice leather binder of information you likely won't read, may not fully understand, and will almost certainly not fully implement. Instead, find a process that includes a simplified model—something easily understood and implemented—that can keep you on track on your way to building wealth. You may find this approach to be less expensive, but more importantly, you will find it more useful.

The analysis of your completed questionnaire and requested documents, in conjunction with the initial planning meeting dialogue, will allow for the creation of your planning model (or summary document).

You and your potential financial advisor should use the initial planning meeting to determine if you have mutual comfort and rapport with before committing to a professional engagement. As such, I believe financial advisors should <u>not</u> charge a fee for the initial meeting. The initial meeting will allow everyone to determine if there is a good fit before getting started, especially since advisor-client relationships should be lifelong and very personal, and you'll want to make sure that everyone is comfortable with one another, and that you are confident in your new financial advisor's ability to provide the guidance you seek.

As advisors, once we have a green light to proceed with the engagement, we build the initial model and narrow down the pile of documents requested and the questionnaire to a four page summary document referred to as our "financial model." I can recall one situation when a prospective client arrived at her first meeting with us with two wheeled suitcases in tow. When those documents were dumped on our conference table, we should have taken a photograph—it was an unbelievable amount of information. However, even in that case we were able to get the four page model to encompass everything we (and she) needed to know about her present planning situation.

Absolutely nothing is included in our model without written verification first. It is unfortunate, but frequently people do not know what they actually own (what type of account, investment, insurance policy, etc . . .) and costly planning mistakes are less likely to be made by clients if we have written proof of each detail of the financial plan in advance of making any recommendations.

Although it is overly simplified below, the primary sections to include in your personal financial model should you wish to do this on your own are as follows:

- Personal data
- Income sources and amounts
- Tax return data
- Risk management and insurance policy information
- Property titles
- Legal documents and responsible parties named in them
- Assets—tangible and intangible
- Liabilities and their terms and conditions
- Beneficiary designations for each applicable account—both primary and contingent
- Action items showing next steps and reminders

Once analysis has begun, you'll need to determine if your plan is on track to reach the goals you've set during the planning process. This can be accomplished in many ways, basically all involving some kind of software, to complete some time value of money calculations. The objective is to determine if the amount of money that you're saving and investing each year is adequate to help you reach financial independence at the age you have set as a target, based upon a set of assumptions for investment returns, inflation, pension and Social Security benefits, etc.

These hypothetical outcome illustrations are useful not only for financial independence and retirement planning, but also for more intermediate-term goals like paying for college educations for your children or grandchildren. Doing the analysis not only allows you to determine if you are on track; it also helps quantify what you would need to do to get on track, if you aren't already there.

*   *   *   *   *

4) Developing and presenting financial planning recommendations and/or alternatives.

In very general terms, the work thus far has been in finding an appropriate advisor, collecting information, and synthesizing it into a manageable format so decisions can be made. With the exception of the federal government, which seems to print money as a solution to virtually any monetary problem, the rest of us have to manage with finite resources. Whether you are a billionaire or you are struggling to make ends meet, the situation is still finite. That means making choices that allocate those resources in a way that matches your priorities.

In some cases, we have seen married couples sacrifice so much to educate their children that they will eventually be forced to live with one of them. When discussing this possible outcome with them, I anecdotally refer to the safety lecture given on commercial airplanes each time they taxi for takeoff. The flight attendant reminds us that in the event of a loss of cabin pressure, oxygen masks will drop from the ceiling and that we are to secure our own masks before helping others with theirs. As a parent, I can't imagine how hard it would be to put on my mask before making sure my daughter was wearing hers. Nonetheless, the advice is sound; if I have no mask and pass out from oxygen deprivation, I can't be of any help to my daughter, and the situation will get decidedly worse for her, too.

The same is true in financial planning. While we all want to help our kids, our grandkids, our parents, and other family members or friends, we are much worse off if we haven't taken care of our own finances first. Once we are financially independent, if we choose to use some of our recurring (albeit finite) resources each year to help others, that is a wonderful thing to be able to do. But until we reach that point, excessive assistance could actually prevent us from ever getting there.

During the recommendation process your advisor will deal with those types of challenges. There are some cases when I can recall telling a family that they can satisfy all of their priorities with their present cash flow. Sadly, this is the exception and not the rule, and most of the time, we have to assist in determining which priorities to fund, and which to delay or eliminate entirely. This is one of many reasons why it is critically important for a couple to be involved in this process together. Your priorities might be different than those of your spouse or partner, and you must communicate together in order for this process to work well.

A list of recommendations will typically be provided as a part of the meeting agenda at your next planning session. Typically, there are several categories of recommendations. In its simplest form, it is a list of things to keep doing, things to do differently, and things to stop doing.

As an example, you advisor might counsel you to keep aggressively paying down consumer debt, to change elections at your next open benefit enrollment at work, and to stop prepaying a mortgage while you have other higher rate non-deductible consumer debt on your balance sheet.

The list can be very long and can take several hours to discuss in detail. However, it is important that before you make any decisions to begin to implement any suggestions, you review the entire plan (either on your own or with your advisor) and that the recommendations are in line with your family's goals and objectives.

*   *   *   *   *

5) Implementing   the   financial   planning
    recommendations.

Thus far, we've talked about medical offices, airline emergencies, and dieticians to describe this process (and no, the financial planning engagement should not be worse than a trip to the dentist). The implementation process has a much more pleasant analogy to go along with it—Thanksgiving dinner.

One of the key elements in preparing Thanksgiving dinner is to try to time the courses so that each is ready simultaneously. If the turkey takes 12 hours and the green beans take 30 minutes, you certainly wouldn't want to start cooking them at the same time.

The same can be said of the financial planning process. Once the recommendations have been reviewed and the initial decisions have been made, we must determine an implementation schedule to make things happen. We usually start with any items that require multiple steps—perhaps underwriting for insurance policies or bank loans, additional third-party advisor involvement (with an attorney, accountant, or other advisor), or specialized paperwork that needs to be obtained through an outside entity (for example, a former employer's human resources department).

If there are insurance applications being completed for life, long-term care, disability or some types of property, casualty, or liability policies, that process can take 45-60 days. Likewise, obtaining credit—an equity line or a mortgage refinance—can take 45-60 days, so you should start with those items that require approval before a final decision can be made.

At the same time, if we are recommending having income tax returns amended and require a CPA's assistance, or we're suggesting the creation or revision of legal or other estate planning documents with an attorney, those can take one to two months, as well, and you'll want to get those processes started early.

If we anticipate consolidation of multiple retirement plans with prior employers, that process generally requires several steps and unique paperwork or follow-up, and you'll want to give that process plenty of time. As some changes may need to coincide with an open enrollment period for employee benefits through an employer, you also need to know when that window is open to make those adjustments.

Once the lengthiest processes have begun, you can begin to handle various types of account transfers or closures, changes to insurance policy benefits or beneficiaries, consolidations or changes to property title—bank accounts, automobiles, etc., and other items that can often take 30 days to complete.

Lastly, once these steps have been taken, you can adjust cash flows (direct deposits or withdrawals), rebalance or redirect investment accounts, and handle the "housekeeping" items that are generally quick and easy relative to the other steps listed above.

The hope is that all of these steps will be completed at the same time so that the plan implementation is as smooth and easy as possible.

Once the implementation has been completed, it is useful to hold a follow-up meeting with two main objectives: 1) to make sure everything you attempted to accomplish was completed properly, and 2) to review all of the accounts, insurance policies, or cash flows to make sure everyone understands what has taken place and is on the same page moving forward.

Anytime paperwork is submitted to a bank, insurance company, investment firm, mortgage lender, or other financial institution, mistakes can occur during implementation. The mistakes can be careless keystroke errors or blatant incompetence, but we *never* assume that when we submit paperwork it is going to be handled accurately.

If you elect to implement on your own, take nothing for granted and verify everything—beneficiaries, account registrations, even your name and address. Significant heartache can be avoided later by making sure that implementation of your financial planning objectives was completed properly at the inception of your planning.

In many cases, you will also get bombarded by statements and confirmations in the mail when you first make some of these adjustments. Much of the mail will be quickly and easily discarded or recycled. However, you will want to keep some of it for your records. If you aren't sure or just want to verify, take the pile of mail that is relevant to your planning to your advisor's office and ask him or her to review it with you to make sure you understand what you own, where it originated, where it is located, and what it is designed to do in your overall plan.

*   *   *   *   *

6) Monitoring the financial planning recommendations.

Once you have completed the initial plan design and have verified the accuracy of your implementation, you will want to get on a regular cycle to review and monitor your progress, to keep you motivated and on track, and to be aware of external factors impacting your planning—tax legislation, interest rates, inflation, market returns, etc.

For most clients, an annual review meeting is sufficient to make adjustments to planning models and hypothetical outcome illustrations for retirement or education projections. You'll also want to keep your advisor updated when there are major changes in your life—financially or otherwise. When changes in your life occur, your plan needs to adjust on the fly. These can be positive changes like marriages, births, job promotions, or windfalls, or they can be negative changes like divorces, deaths, job losses, illnesses, accidents, and the like.

Likewise, your advisor will need to keep you up to date throughout the year when opportunities or challenges present themselves. This is not to suggest that your advisor should react to market volatility by trying to "time" markets, as we'd never suggest such an endeavor. However, events or trends that could change the results of your plan require some level of attention and need to be communicated to you.

The extent to which you and your advisor communicate will vary based upon the type of advisory firm you use, the complexity of your financial world, and your personal preferences.

Now that you have a sense of the overall process, let's get started.

CHAPTER THREE

TAKING INVENTORY

WHERE YOU'RE GOING BEGINS WITH KNOWING WHERE YOU ARE

While envisioning our destination is always exciting, the first step in any journey is determining the launch point. This helps us explore various trajectories and ultimately to decide on an optimal path from A to B. Financial planning is no different.

Here are seven things you need to measure before you start making any changes to your financial plan:

1) Do you have positive or negative cash flow?
2) Do you have adverse debt?
3) Do you know your net worth?
4) Do you know your *liquid* net worth?
5) Do you have a suitable emergency fund?
6) Do you have contingency planning in place?
7) Have you set your planning goals and objectives and do you know if you are on track to meet or exceed them?

At first glance, you will notice that absent from this list are questions dealing with any specifics—about portfolio holdings or design, insurance products, investment philosophy, or the institutions you use for banking, investing, or insuring. That is because those details are not nearly as important to the success of a plan as the basics. Owning a hot mutual fund or stock is not the same as having a financial plan. Neither is having a fixed mortgage versus an adjustable one, owning gold bars, or using whole life insurance. All of these are tools, but they are also the *noise* that can prevent people from making plans. Sometimes it can seem too overwhelming to fight through that noise, so inertia sets in and no progress is made.

For now, let's talk about the foundations—these seven questions—and then we'll come back to the specific tools that can help make a plan a reality.

1) Do you have positive or negative cash flow?

"Cash flow" is the illustration of money being earned and money being spent. If you are spending more than you are earning, you have a fundamental problem that needs to be addressed before any planning can be done. Think of it as plugging the hole in the bottom of your bucket before trying to fill it up.

There are several solutions to this problem, and on the surface they are obvious: make more money and/or spend less money. However, it is rarely that simple. While you could seek a promotion or a new job, or you could take a second job, it is rare that major income increases happen overnight. It may be that going back to school to learn new skills or to finish your degree could lead to higher earning potential, and that is an excellent way to do it, but it will take significant time and will require some planning (not to mention the possibility of some tuition expenses!)

It may also be that you can increase your income in a more passive way—by investing in income-producing bank accounts or securities, for example. If you have funds in a savings account earning 0.25% and can move them to a certificate of deposit earning 2.0% it will create more income. Of course, it may also create a lack of liquidity or fees and penalties if used incorrectly. It is also not likely to change your negative cash flow into positive cash flow by itself. Likewise, investing for income (or yield) can be a suitable strategy for some investors but not for others. In fact, some financial vehicles may be more (or less) appropriate for your specific needs for a variety of possible reasons beyond the scope of this book.

As it is often difficult to increase your income overnight in an amount suitable to change a cash flow imbalance, you'll need to look at what you are spending and try to make some meaningful change in that area. Notice, I have yet to use the word *budget*. That is because the word sends the same chills up our spines as *root canal* does. While I am not suggesting that you impose a strict budget upon yourself, I do suggest that you *track* where the money is going and aim to make meaningful changes where you can. It might mean refinancing a debt or eating in restaurants less frequently, or it might mean curtailing a habit related to shopping or $4 cups of coffee. It might also mean looking for less expensive housing options or automobiles or exploring public school options rather than private school options for kids.

Every situation is unique, and once you track your expenses, you'll have a better idea of where the money is going. Again, I suggest Quicken™ as a software solution, but pen and paper work just fine too, as long as you are diligent.

*   *   *   *   *

2) Do you have adverse debt?

No discussion about wealth building can be complete without a discussion on debt. In brief, debt is a great leveler of dreams and costs a lot of American families a lot of sleep at night. In the simplest of terms, if you can't afford something, *don't buy it.* I know that will be lousy for the U.S. economy in terms of consumer confidence and output by retailers and manufacturers, but your own economic recovery from debt must come first. If you can't afford it, *don't buy it.*

Needless to say, not all debt is *bad debt.* A mortgage on a home, rental property, or office building creates leverage and can be a good way to buy an asset that becomes the collateral and allows for financing. Student loans can be acceptable debt if the terms are favorable and if your degree results in higher earning potential for a lifetime. However, credit cards, department store cards, and other consumer debt are categorically *bad debt* and should be avoided as much as possible. Even car loans should be avoided (or postponed as long as possible) and should only be undertaken if the resulting payment won't too adversely impact your cash flow or render your savings and investment goals moot.

If it is appropriate for you and your family to review a detailed discussion on debt, I encourage you to refer to my last book, *"Debt-Free for Life: The Tools You Need to Free Yourself from Debt."* In it you will find lots of detailed tips for getting out of debt and staying out of debt so you can begin the wealth building journey we're about to undertake in this volume.

*   *   *   *   *

3) Do you know your net worth?

Your net worth is a relatively simple calculation. To reach it, you add up all of your assets and then subtract all of your liabilities. If your house is worth $500,000 and you have a mortgage balance of $200,000, it will add $300,000 to your net worth. Your assets include everything you own—houses, bank accounts, investment accounts, cash value in your life insurance, retirement plans, artwork, jewelry, etc. Likewise, your liabilities include everything you owe—mortgages, equity lines, car loans, student loans, credit cards, margin loans, etc.

One of the key objectives in financial planning is to calculate the amount of money you need to save to retire. Before trying to determine your *target* net worth, you need to identify your *current* net worth. Like the *"You are here"* sticker on a mall kiosk map, in order to get where you're going, you've first got to establish where you are.

As you become wealthier, knowing your net worth becomes increasingly important, primarily for tax purposes. When you and your spouse or partner die, before assets can be distributed to your children or other heirs, the government steps in with their calculators and decides how much of your property to confiscate prior to allowing the next generation to enjoy it. If this sounds harsh and a bit ridiculous, it is. Nonetheless, the federal government and many state governments have their hands in your pockets beyond the grave. With careful estate planning you can eliminate or offset this risk, and we'll talk a bit later about selecting an attorney who can assist you with this process.

For the purposes of this section, just know that under current law, the federal government does not tax the first $5,000,000 left behind by each individual, and that most states or other jurisdictions do not tax the first $1,000,000 left behind by each individual.

While those numbers sound large enough to exclude most households, because the death benefits paid by life insurance count in the calculation, these taxes actually impact more households than you might suspect.

The rules are very complicated and change constantly, so you'll need to make sure that you have a qualified estate planning attorney to work with you and your financial advisor to mitigate this potential taxation as much as possible.

*   *   *   *   *

4) Do you know your *liquid* net worth?

I consider this question to be more important than the last for most families. That is because liquid net worth measures the resources that can be used to create spendable income right away, whereas the overall net worth includes those resources that might require encumbrance or sale before they can create income, and that might take time, cost money, or be impossible to accomplish for various reasons.

For people over age 55, liquid net worth is generally all of your net property <u>not including</u> your primary residence, closely-held business interests, or vacation real estate. For younger people, we generally also exclude retirement plans from a liquid net worth calculation, as they cannot be utilized favorably at that time. Even for people aged 55-59 ½, there are restrictions on the use of qualified retirement accounts and IRAs, and, therefore, we may exclude them from a calculation unless "early retirement" is being seriously considered.

Choosing a sustainable withdrawal rate (defined as a percentage of your working assets which you can withdrawal each year without placing so much pressure on your principal as to risk running out of money) is a very important and challenging task. I have seen lots of so-called "Monte Carlo simulations" for retirees which illustrate the odds of outliving their money, and which show a perfect scenario until age 87, but with complete poverty awaiting them on their 88th birthday. To me, that is not sound planning. Although our present health, family history, and personal habits may provide some indication, we do not definitively know how long we're going to live. Thus, to me the only plan that makes sense is one that provides for adequate resources throughout the human life span and that is most likely to leave funds behind for heirs or charities.

There are many schools of thought on withdrawal rates. These rates reflect the percentage of annual withdrawals taken against a principal sum, irrespective of whether there are enough earnings or growth to warrant that withdrawal over each period. In other words, if a withdrawal rate is four percent, for every $1,000,000 in liquid net worth (sometimes referred to as "working assets") there will be $40,000 in withdrawals taken from that account each year. In an ideal world, to be more comfortable regarding the likelihood of maintaining a lifetime of principal, a rate of three percent would be used. However, in our planning with clients, the world is seldom ideal. Any withdrawal rate higher than five percent causes me a great deal of concern as an advisor.

When undertaking planning for sustainable wealth, we will only use those assets that will predictably be working assets (i.e., the liquid net worth figure) in determining the answer to the question, "How much do I need to retire?"

We'll talk more about that calculation later in this chapter.

* * * * *

5) Do you have a suitable emergency fund?

In the grand scheme of things, having an emergency fund of readily available cash is an important step towards financial independence. It is also a good way to make sure you aren't losing sleep at night. I've seen the required size of that emergency fund articulated in various rules of thumb by the media and other professionals and organizations. However, I consider rules of thumb to be dangerous as planning tools because every situation is unique and one size never fits all.

In general terms, for households with dual incomes (when the two incomes are similarly sized), we tend to use three months of expenditures, net of taxes, as the emergency fund target. For a household with only one income, or with enough income disparity that there is a clear breadwinner, we tend to use six months as a barometer.

The reason for this difference is that while it is possible to insure against many risks in our planning which will be discussed in the next chapter, we cannot effectively insure against loss of a job. Unemployment benefits are inadequate for most households, so resources will need to be available during a period of unemployment or underemployment. If the breadwinner becomes unemployed, it is a serious blow to the household. If one of two equal breadwinners becomes unemployed, it requires only half of the emergency fund draw, which means that three months of overall net expenditures can last for six months if only half of the amount required to pay the bills is taken from the fund each month.

For retirees, we will often set the emergency fund target higher—as much as one to two years of expenditures—to make sure that in volatile market conditions or interest rate environments, big decisions can be postponed or timed to minimize the need for selling securities at an adverse time to cover monthly expenses in retirement.

Your situation will be unique in all ways, including this one, so if your personal circumstances or comfort level vary from these ranges, let your advisor know and your plan can be adjusted accordingly. The risk of maintaining too small an emergency fund is clear—the need for immediate capital may require transactions, fees, taxes, or penalties if there isn't enough easily accessible cash. On the other hand, the risk in maintaining too large an emergency fund is more of a hidden cost—the *opportunity cost*—which means that you are sacrificing possible opportunities for returns in exchange for a larger cash holding. Naturally, you're also minimizing the risk of loss of principal with those funds, which is why I maintain that every situation is unique and "rules of thumb" are insufficient rationales for financial decision-making.

We'll talk more about where to hold an emergency fund in Chapter Four.

*   *   *   *   *

6) Do you have contingency planning in place?

In the next chapter, we are going to discuss risk management in depth. For now, understand that the only *ideal* financial plan is one which works *no matter what*. If there is unemployment, illness, disability, premature death, lawsuit, divorce, extreme longevity and/or cognitive impairment, the plan *must* be prepared to handle it. Otherwise, the plan is set to fail under various circumstances and isn't ideal.

There will be reasons why people choose not to take all of the risk management steps we suggest. Some of them are legitimate limitations based on individual circumstances, while others seem to be rationalizations. However, it is your advisor's job to inform and yours to decide. Should you elect to self-insure or ignore various contingency plans, you are accepting a risk instead of passing it to an insurer, and the plan will only be a good one as long as that risk is avoided or its impact is minimized.

* * * * *

7) Have you set your planning goals and objectives and do you know if you are on track to meet or exceed them?

So you have your current net worth statement, you've completed your contingency planning, and you have positive cash flow to support your wealth creation efforts. You may even know your target net worth for retirement. But do you know if you are on track to get there within the timeframe you'd like?

Depending on your age and income level, you are likely to find that your target net worth is larger than you ever imagined. That is because the impact that inflation has on the value of a dollar is extreme and future dollars are worth less than current ones. Thus, it takes far more of them just to maintain your present lifestyle in the future.

As a simple example, if you determine that you need $100,000 per year in today's dollars to replace your income (net of savings but before the impact of taxes), and plan to retire in 25 years, here are the numbers:

In today's dollars, with a five percent maximum withdrawal rate, you would need $2,000,000 to create $100,000 per year. However, if we adjust for a hypothetical 3.5% inflation rate, the $100,000 per year in 25 years is actually $236,324 *per year.* With that same maximum five percent withdrawal rate, it means you would need $4,726,480 in principal to withdraw the $236,324 in your first year of retirement 25 years from now to live *exactly* as you could on $100,000 today.

Of course there is more to the calculation than that simple example, but the point of that exercise is to show the impact of inflation on your target net worth and why it sounds so big. In that example, if you had $3,000,000 in working assets *today* (less than your target number of $4,726,480) and only needed $100,000 per year to live comfortably, you would be "wealthy" based on our definition and would likely not need to work another day in your life.

On the other hand, using your five percent withdrawal assumption, having that same $3,000,000 in working assets *25 years from now* would mean having only $150,000 of your targeted $236,324 annual lifestyle. That means you'd have only 63% of your pre-retirement income and would either have to work part-time to close the gap, adjust your lifestyle dramatically, or postpone retirement for potentially a long time.

So, if the person in that example reached $3,000,000 in working assets today, he or she is *wealthy* based on our definition in Chapter One, whereas reaching that same figure in 25 years has that person unprepared to retire. We'll address strategies for how to close the gap between your *current* retirement projection and an *ideal* one later in the book.

Now that you have a sense of how big your target net worth might be, let's dig into the planning. We'll start with the risk management elements of your contingency plan, which must be in place before any significant wealth building makes sense.

CHAPTER FOUR

RISK MANAGEMENT

ELEVEN COMMON DEFENSIVE TOOLS TO HELP YOU AVOID THE PITFALLS THAT CAN DERAIL FINANCIAL PLANS

In medieval times, wealthy families built elaborate castles to protect and display their wealth. They were built with moats and other defensive mechanisms in an attempt to protect the people and property inside from potential thieves or other unsavory characters.

While today's world is significantly different, you will still want to do additional research or to discuss the appropriate risk management tools with your financial advisor so that the moat around your proverbial castle is wide enough and deep enough to protect your loved ones and valued property.

Not all of the defensive vehicles involve insurance, although insurance is a readily accessible risk management tool. The purpose of insurance is to transfer risk which you cannot afford to bear. It is too expensive to insure against everything that can go wrong in life, so it is better to identify the big risks and trade them in for predictable premiums. In other words, you don't need to use insurance for an annoying door ding on your car, but you will need to have insurance in case you are in a major accident.

Here is a list of eleven of the primary types of defensive tools you'll want to have working for you, as appropriate, in your planning:

1. Emergency Fund + Liquidity
2. Automobile Insurance
3. Homeowners/Renters Insurance
4. Liability Insurance—both personal and professional
5. Disability Insurance
6. Long-Term Care Insurance
7. Medical Insurance
8. Life Insurance
9. Estate Planning Documents
10. Asset Titling
11. Beneficiary Designations

Let's explore each of these in detail.

1. Emergency Fund + Liquidity

The concept of an emergency (or "rainy-day") fund is fairly commonplace, and yet very few households I encounter actually have such a fund. Moreover, those that do have an emergency fund have no idea how to quantify the fund beyond "an amount that helps them sleep at night."

While a good night's sleep is an excellent goal, the purpose of an emergency fund is to have available liquid capital when crises arise without the need to make decisions that are expensive to execute. When I talk to clients about the moat around their financial castle, the very first (outward-most) layer of defense is the emergency fund.

An emergency fund can take many forms. In its simplest incarnation, it would simply be a savings or money market account holding immediately-available liquid capital. During times when money market accounts are paying five percent interest that may be all the line of defense you need. However, as of this writing, most money market accounts are paying less than one percent interest and some savings accounts are paying basically no interest at all.

Thus, while it is important to have some cash in a readily-available account like a savings or money market account, it is also appropriate to hold some of your emergency fund in assets that have a potentially better rate of return, like a certificate of deposit, or CD.[1] As long as the CD has no penalty for early termination, you only need to hold one CD at your local bank or at a national or even online institution. However, if you would face a stiff penalty for early withdrawal, you might need to hold a series of CDs, potentially with staggered maturity (or liquidity) dates to avoid an expensive problem if you needed to access a lot of capital relatively quickly.

It may also be appropriate, if you have enough equity in your home, to maintain a home equity line-of-credit (or HELOC) against your house. If you have a HELOC with a $0 balance, there should be no cost to maintain it. However, it is nice to have a checkbook that can access capital immediately in an emergency, and the HELOC allows you to draw against the line and then to repay it, either at once or over time, with funds from your remaining assets or your income. It usually provides a much lower rate of interest than revolving consumer debt like a credit card, and the interest may be tax-deductible. You'll want to check with your CPA or tax-preparer to be sure you can deduct this interest, as only those taxpayers taking advantage of itemized deductions (as opposed to the standard deduction) can qualify, and some other limits regarding the use of the borrowed funds also apply.

Another place to turn for quick liquidity is the cash value in permanent life insurance policies. We'll discuss this vehicle later in the book in greater detail, but if you have cash available and need it in a crunch, it can often be accessed as a loan.

If your savings and money market accounts are your first line of defense and your HELOC or life insurance cash value is your second line of defense, your third line of defense will be your non-qualified investment accounts (accounts which are not qualified retirement plans or various types of IRAs). The reason that these accounts can assist in an emergency is that the return of principal in these accounts is not taxable to you, so you would only pay a capital gains tax (at a favorable tax rate as of this writing) and only on the amount of your gain, if any, when you make a withdrawal. On the other hand, with only a few exceptions, a withdrawal from a qualified retirement plan or IRA prior to age 59 ½ will result in significant taxes and penalties. Non-qualified investment accounts are a relatively easy and inexpensive place to get capital if you need it quickly.

One final thought about types of emergency funds. While credit cards are a convenient way to spend, and to earn points towards various benefits, if possible, you will want to avoid using credit cards to handle larger financial emergencies, because they often have high, non-deductible interest rates and can get you into trouble quickly. Moreover, avoid at all costs taking a loan against a 401(k) or other retirement plan. There is no more expensive place to get funds than that for various tax reasons, and a plan loan should be seen as a very last resort.

*   *   *   *   *

Now that we have discussed where to hold an emergency fund, let's talk about *how much* to hold in one.

Like we discussed in the last chapter, as your household expenses increase, the size of your ideal emergency fund typically increases as well. That is because in a period without your income due to job loss or an injury or illness that creates an income reduction, your bills will not stop coming just because your paychecks do.

As a simple example, if your household bills are $8,000 per month, you will need to have enough of an emergency fund to cover your expenses for a period of time. The length of that period depends on whether your household relies on a single-income or dual-income and how secure you feel about your income sources.

If you are self-employed and therefore cannot be fired, you may feel a sense of job security that you wouldn't feel if you could be subject to a pink slip at any time. Of course, the flipside of that equation is that if you are self-employed, your income can vary widely based on the revenues and expenses of your enterprise.

If you determine that six months of expenses is an appropriate emergency fund, in the example above with $8,000 in monthly expenses, you would want to maintain a $48,000 emergency fund. It would be reasonable to hold $24,000 (or three months' worth) in a savings or money market account and the other $24,000 in a CD or similar vehicle to try to get a better return on the funds. It would also help to have another $48,000 in available credit on a HELOC, bringing the total available capital up to $96,000 without the need to sell securities, (potentially at an adverse time), to use a credit card for financing, or to take premature distributions from a qualified plan to cover the emergency. The availability of the HELOC effectively provides an additional layer of protection to double the size of the cash emergency fund. The reason I like to see the cash emergency fund doubled is that after an "emergency" which depletes the cash, available credit can be very helpful during the time needed to rebuild the cash fund in the event there is a subsequent emergency.

A few more comments about emergency funds, before we move on:

- They can also be "opportunity funds" and should be considered as available capital for certain types of opportunities that life presents at times.

- They can also be used for major events or purchases like a new car or a family vacation, as long as there are defined plans to repay the fund. Instead of paying interest to a car dealership and making payments to them, you would be making the same payments back to your own emergency (or opportunity) fund.

- Lastly, since the fund is designed to pay bills over time during a period of reduced income, the amount of capital that you can access in a *single day* rarely needs to be the full amount of the emergency fund. The only exception I can even contemplate when all of the funds would be needed at once is bail, and here's hoping that is never a consideration in your household!

*   *   *   *   *

2. Automobile Insurance

There are many different kinds of coverage which fall under the name "property and casualty insurance." For most families, the two most prevalent are automobile insurance and homeowners' (or renters') insurance. While there are additional features of boat, RV, and motorcycle insurance, and other less common types, we are going to focus on the big two.

For most Americans, the most dangerous activity in which we participate (at least regularly) is driving. There are few greater sources of damage or liability than when we get behind the wheel of our cars or trucks. As a result, the proper coverage is critical to protecting our financial well-being. Laws vary from state to state, but generally, the state-imposed minimum coverage level is insufficient to cover the risks we face when driving.

There are three primary limits on automobile insurance that define the amount of coverage provided by your policy and they can be found on the "declarations page." The first is a property limit, the second is a liability limit (generally for your actions and for those of uninsured or underinsured drivers with whom you come into contact), and the third is your retention limit (or deductible) for both comprehensive and collision claims.

Property limits are designed to cover the physical value of the automobiles involved in an accident. While these are important, the far larger threat to your financial security is found under the liability section, which covers you in the event of a lawsuit stemming from an incident while you or a family member is driving your car. In some states, the minimum liability coverage is $50,000 or so. However, when someone is injured or killed in an auto accident, they (or their family members) don't sue for $50,000. They often sue for millions of dollars.

I generally suggest at least $500,000 of liability coverage, as well as a property limit of $100,000 on these policies.

The deductible amount is the amount that is not paid by the insurance company in the event of a claim and is paid out of your pocket before any insurance proceeds are paid. For most people, a $250 deductible is reasonable for comprehensive claims (resulting from dings and scratches and cracked windshields), and a $500 or $1,000 deductible is suitable for collision claims (resulting from an auto accident). The higher you set your deductible, the lower your premium, but also the higher amount you'll be required to pay towards a claim before any financial benefit is derived from the coverage.

As automobile insurance usually renews automatically each year, it is a good idea to explore a few insurance carriers periodically to make sure you have a competitive policy and premium. If you have any accidents or tickets on your record, it can be difficult or expensive to change carriers. Note that there are some insurers who will insure only preferred risk drivers (i.e. those drivers with the best records). If that describes you and your family, you'll want to be with one of those companies, if possible, to get the best available coverage at the most competitive rate. Lastly, when you have teenage drivers in your household, you can expect your premiums to be very high and may want to get rate quotes from multiple insurance carriers, as some will cover teenage drivers more favorably than others.

* * * * *

3. Homeowners'/Renters' Insurance

The two primary types of insurance for your home and personal property are homeowners' insurance (if you own your home) and renters' insurance (if you are a tenant).

Renters' insurance is only designed to cover your personal property and to provide a liability limit for you. You do not need to insure the physical structure, as the owner of the house or apartment must do that. Property limits will vary widely depending on the value of your belongings (furniture, televisions, clothing, etc.) but generally should be a high enough number that in the event of a disaster you can replace everything you own and start over.

Homeowners' insurance will vary based on whether your home is a single-family house, a townhouse, or a condominium.

In a single-family house or townhouse, normally if you have a mortgage, as a part of your monthly payment your mortgage company will require you to make a deposit into your escrow account each month to fund your homeowners' insurance policy premiums annually. They want to make sure that you have paid your premium because they don't want to see the collateral backing their loan to you destroyed without proper protection.

Your homeowners' policy will have three primary areas insured—dwelling, property, and liability. The dwelling is the physical structure of the house. It needs to be insured at a level such that if there were a total loss, you could have the structure rebuilt. The dwelling limit does not necessarily need to be as high as the fair market value of your property, because you are not insuring the land upon which the dwelling is built; you are only insuring the dwelling itself.

The most important feature of a homeowners' dwelling coverage is to make sure that you have "full replacement cost" coverage. That way, if the insurance company recommends you to maintain $200,000 of coverage, but it costs $300,000 to rebuild your home, it becomes the insurance company's problem and not yours. Without full replacement cost coverage, you could accidentally be setting yourself up for a large "deductible" when you have to pay the overage amount ($100,000 in the example above) out of pocket, in the event of a claim.

Note that policies often have very important exclusions that may require you to buy additional endorsements or even separate policies. For example, most policies will *not* cover damage by flood, and many will exclude hurricanes, tornados, and the like depending where you live. If you are in an area defined as a "flood plain," you'll need to explore federal flood insurance in addition to your homeowners' policy. There are other exclusions that are company-specific or state-specific, so read the policy very closely and ask your agent as many questions as necessary to make sure you have the protection you need.

The property coverage under a homeowners' policy is similar to that of a renters' policy—the value of your "stuff." One note of caution about the property coverage—many policies have limits on certain types of property like artwork, jewelry, and collectibles. If you have any of these items in your home worth in excess of $3,000, you'll want to get excess "scheduled personal property coverage" under your policy and to have each item appraised and listed by name and value line-by-line on your declaration page. Some companies will include the scheduled personal property coverage in the same homeowners' policy, while other companies will write it as a separate policy (called "inland marine coverage") with its own declaration page.

While lots of endorsements are typically available to add to your homeowners' or renters' policy, the one that you will want to accept regardless of your personal situation is the rider for identity theft and fraud. In rare instances, this coverage may be in the basic policy, but with most companies you have to add it as an additional coverage. These riders are very inexpensive ($25-50 per year), but they can save the day if you're are a victim of identity theft or a similar crime by assigning a case manager to help you navigate a very complicated and frustrating process and by providing funds for lost wages or travel expenses incurred in cleaning up your fraud-damaged credit.

There are some very tricky and important rules if you own a condominium, and you'll want a copy of the master policy to find out what is covered by the condo association and what you need to cover on your own. Generally, anything inside your walls is your responsibility and anything from the walls outward is the responsibility of the master policy. However, imagine the situation where you live on the 2nd floor of a condo building and your icemaker leaks and floods your neighbor's unit on the floor below. You need to make sure that you are protected, so ask the tough questions of your insurance agent.

Make sure to discuss amendments and alterations coverage if you upgraded anything in your unit— carpet, cabinets, fixtures, etc., as the master policy might only cover contractor-grade fixtures. Ask whether your policy covers the master policy deductible in the event that a loss starts in your unit and impacts one or more of your neighbors' units. That deductible can be $10,000 or more and that can be a very expensive and unpleasant surprise down the road.

Like the automobile policy, your homeowners' policy will have a deductible, which you can set. The higher your deductible is, the lower your premium will be. For some homeowners, a deductible of $500 or $1,000 will be necessary. However, if you have significant cash reserves, consider a deductible of $2,500, or even 1% of your dwelling coverage, to lower your premium. You'll want to avoid filing small claims, as they can impact your premium rating. Better to deal with the small events out of pocket and to keep the insurance for the big things. Remember: the primary purpose of insurance is to pass risks you *cannot* bear.

For liability limits on both homeowners' and condominium policies, I suggest that the limit be high enough to allow you to add excess liability insurance (discussed below), so check with your agent and find out that limit—it is usually either $100,000 or $250,000, but it can be higher.

*　　*　　*　　*　　*

4. Liability Insurance

We have already discussed the liability limits that will be included in your automobile and homeowners' insurance policies. However, one of the biggest risks to financial security is the risk of being named in a lawsuit. One way to protect yourself and your family is with an excess liability umbrella policy. As the name implies, the umbrella policy goes over and above your home and car coverage. The umbrella is bought in increments of $1,000,000 and is relatively inexpensive (because it only provides coverage once the liability limits of the homeowners' or auto policy have been exhausted).

I generally recommend $1,000,000 as a baseline, and then the policy can grow as your net worth grows. These policies are not only for the wealthy. They can also be useful for families with high income, even if their net worth is modest. A large lawsuit can decimate you in two ways financially—one is having your assets used to pay a claim, and the other is having your wages attached to pay a judgment, which is a risk worth insuring at almost any income level.

Talk to your insurance agent or company who handles your home and auto coverage about adding a liability umbrella policy. Often, to obtain an umbrella policy, you must have all three policies with the same company. As a rule, carriers provide multi-policy discounts, so keeping all of your "property and casualty" insurance with the same company is usually a good idea, whether you opt for the umbrella or not.

*   *   *   *   *

5. Disability Insurance

If you had a goose that could lay golden eggs, would you insure only the golden eggs, or would you also insure the goose? We just talked at length about insuring your property. However, for working people, the largest single financial risk that can decimate savings and create debt or insolvency the fastest, is to become suddenly unable to work. While none of us like to picture ourselves unable to work, illnesses and injuries are a fact of life, and we need to be as prepared as we can, even if we hope we never need the coverage.

For many working Americans, disability insurance is provided through their employers in a group policy. Typically, there are two types of disability coverage— short-term disability (STD) and long-term disability (LTD).

STD benefits are usually limited to 90 days or 180 days and are designed to provide a paycheck while you recover from an illness or injury. Some STD policies will also provide benefits during maternity leave. These policies are usually employer-paid group benefits or individually-paid voluntary benefits. Benefits are usually paid weekly and are capped at either a dollar amount or a percentage of salary. A typical limit is 60% of your salary up to $1,000 per week. The benefits are generally free from income tax, because any premiums paid are not tax deductible.

LTD is by far the more important of the two coverage types for most individuals to carry. That is because LTD is designed to replace a portion of your income for many years. Like STD policies, the benefits under LTD are usually capped at 60% of your salary up to a set limit (often $5,000 or $10,000 per month). Most policies will provide monthly benefits up to a dollar limit or salary percentage until age 65 or for five years, whichever is longer. It is very important to pay premiums with after-tax dollars (i.e. not to take a tax deduction) so that benefits paid in the event of a claim will be free of income tax.

For people without group disability policies through their employers, or for people with income in excess of a group policy's benefit limit, individual policies can be obtained. The process usually requires full medical and financial underwriting, including a paramedical exam and a review of your recent paycheck and one to two years of your tax returns.

For professionals, it is very important to get coverage that defines being disabled in terms of being unable to engage in your *own occupation*. This language can be found in the definitions section of a disability policy and is perhaps the most important paragraph in the whole policy. If you are a surgeon or a concert pianist, you could literally become fully disabled by slamming your hand in a car door if it kept you from performing surgery or playing the piano. If the contract has language about "any occupation," you are only disabled if you can't work at all in any job, often with little regard as to how much your income has been reduced.

Lastly, if you are buying a policy for yourself, there is another important distinction regarding the policy premiums, which can be very tricky. If a policy is "guaranteed renewable," it means that you cannot have it cancelled by the insurance company except for your failure to pay a premium. However, it does *not* mean that your premium amount is guaranteed to remain the same. To have a premium that cannot be increased by the insurance company, the policy must be "non-cancellable and guaranteed renewable." This is a question to ask your financial advisor or insurance agent, to make sure you know exactly what the insurance company can and cannot do with your premium rates.

Since benefits are generally not taxable, if you are able to get 60-70% of your income insured, that is usually enough for LTD.

*   *   *   *   *

6. Long-Term Care Insurance [2]

On the surface, long-term care insurance (LTCI) is perhaps the least appealing of the risk management tools we're going to discuss. That is because it is hard to imagine what our lives might be like if we were to become unable to take care of ourselves, either in our advanced years or due to an accident or illness. Most people mistakenly think of long-term care insurance as "elder care" insurance or "nursing home" coverage. While there are ample examples to merit those misconceptions, you do not have to be elderly to have a claim, nor do you have to be confined to a nursing home under most policies.

LTCI is designed to cover some of the enormous costs involved in caring for an individual who is unable to perform "activities of daily living" or ADLs. Generally, claims fall into two categories—one is cognitive (for someone who develops Alzheimer's disease or other impairment), and the other is physical (for someone frail or incapacitated). To have a claim, usually an insured must be unable to perform two of the six ADLs as defined by the contract. These are typically listed as bathing, dressing, eating, transferring (from bed to chair or chair to bed), toileting, and continence.

The two primary reasons why people do not buy LTCI (other than cost, if it is prohibitive) are that they believe their children will care for them or that they are expecting to die quickly and naturally and never need it.

In all reality, even with supportive children, people are not thinking about the realities of caring for a disabled person. It is one thing to have your kids stop by to bring you lunch or help with paying your bills, and another thing entirely to have them come to the house to give you a bath or to help you use the toilet. None of us wants to be in that condition, but if we are, we certainly don't want to burden our children with our care. Besides, in most cases, adult children have jobs and families of their own, and they often live out of town.

LTCI is designed to provide either a daily or a monthly benefit for a set period of years in the event of a claim. While it is too complex to go into all of the details in this limited space, in general there are a few things to consider when exploring a policy:

- Monthly benefits are preferable to daily ones when you have to file a claim because your use of medical services can vary widely day-to-day. Depending where you live, a typical monthly benefit may be $6,000 per month or more.

- Some contracts are *indemnity* contracts, while others are *reimbursement* contracts. An indemnity contract will pay the full monthly benefit every month, even if the entire benefit isn't "spent" on care. A reimbursement contract will only pay the actual amount of the claims filed, and any unused benefit will usually remain in the contract in a benefit pool, which could extend the length of the contractual benefit period.

- There are meaningful discounts for married people who both apply together, as well as for unmarried partners who live together in some states.

- Policies can be structured to allow benefits to be shared so that either spouse or partner can use them. In these cases, I normally suggest four years of benefits per person (or eight combined). If you are unmarried, a five or six year contract just for yourself might be more appropriate than four years.

- Inflation protection is crucial to this product, especially for people under 70-75 years old who obtain it. As the cost of care goes up, it is critical that the benefits in the policy go up as well.

- Premiums are *not* guaranteed. Unlike some disability policies we discussed, there is no such thing as a guaranteed premium LTCI policy as of this writing. There are ways to pay for policies fully in a set number of years rather than paying premiums forever, or to pay for policies with a lump-sum asset transfer, but otherwise premiums can (and I believe *will*) increase over time with the cost of medical care.

- There are lots of available "bells and whistles" in some of these policies, and they are often a waste of money. Buy insurance to pass risk you cannot bear, but do not become insurance-poor by buying the extras and add-ons.

- Traditional health insurance *does not* cover long-term care expenses, and Medicare only provides a small benefit for up to 100 days and only for certain types of care.

- LTCI is *not* only for the elderly. A perfect example of that is Christopher Reeve, (who played the lead role in the "Superman" movies in the 1970s and, as an otherwise perfectly healthy adult, was paralyzed in an accident that caused him to spend his last few years largely incapacitated).

- LTCI is more affordable if you are young and healthy and gets much more expensive if you wait until you are older or less healthy to obtain it. However, because premiums are not guaranteed and can increase, there is also risk in obtaining the coverage at too young an age, unless the policy has some provision to be fully paid-up at some specified future date.

- Some relatively new (as of this writing) forms of LTCI have been introduced by insurance companies trying to make the product more attractive and also trying to cap their downside risk in issuing the coverage. One such form is a life insurance policy rider that allows the insured person to spend his or her own death benefit gradually for long-term care expenses, if needed. These policies were traditionally like houseboats—you could live on them and could travel on them, but they weren't great as houses and they weren't great as boats! Today, that is changing and there are reasons why, especially for unmarried or widowed people with children, a hybrid between life insurance and LTCI might be useful as a tool. [3]

- Two kinds of people do not need LTCI—those who are nearly Medicaid-qualified and basically bankrupt, and those who are so wealthy that a claim would be irrelevant to their financial security. For the rest of the population, it is a key component to our risk management and financial plans.

While we have barely scratched the surface on LTCI, the bottom line is that it is a huge financial risk and that a disabled person can quickly bankrupt a healthy spouse, partner, or other family members without the right insurance coverage.

7. Medical Insurance

As of this writing, it is difficult to pick up a newspaper or turn on the television news without hearing about the state of healthcare in the U.S. and all of the politicking taking place in the federal and state governments. While this is not a forum for political discussion, I will attempt to provide a brief summary of the health insurance world as we know it currently.

Medical insurance is dominated by a model that is employer-centric. That means that in most cases, someone must have an employer who offers coverage to obtain it favorably and without personal underwriting. For better or worse, that means that when you are looking for a job or making a career move, the employee benefits (including health insurance) may be as important as the discussion about salary or wages.

Medical insurance tends to be very expensive if you obtain it on your own or if you work for a for-profit company. Only those employed by the government or by extremely benevolent private companies can get medical insurance without it being an onerous expense for their family. The newly formed health insurance exchanges are likely to make individual health insurance more readily accessible and easier to obtain, but there is no telling what the impact on premiums will be, and I suspect that further government involvement in healthcare will not make it less expensive.

That being said, it is so important to have health insurance that I can't imagine any single risk management item that would precede it if we were to rank them in some way. While even uninsured individuals have access to emergency and hospital care, it is very uncommon for the uninsured to be able to get favorable access to physicians or preventative care.

If your employer offers health insurance benefits, I urge you to accept them. If there are multiple plan offerings, read them carefully and ask your financial advisor or benefits coordinator to help you select one. If your employer does not offer you coverage, explore individually underwritten plans or state-mandated plans to make sure you have at least catastrophic coverage. In the U.S., many bankruptcies are declared each year due to a medical situation, and health insurance can help you avoid being part of that troubling statistical group.

*   *   *   *   *

8. Life Insurance[4]

There are few insurance products that are as misunderstood as life insurance. I believe that the insurance industry and the hordes of agents and brokers selling it have made life insurance more confusing than it needs to be. While there are lots of wealth creation, preservation, and transfer strategies and lots of creative tax and business planning uses for life insurance, for the purposes of this reference, I want to keep it as simple as possible.

On a fundamental level, life insurance is designed to replace the "human life value" of someone who dies. For a working person, that means that life insurance can be structured to make sure that your paychecks keep coming to your family, even if you are deceased.

As a rule, someone young and single (without children) does not need life insurance. There are lots of reasons why they might *want* life insurance, but they do not *need* it. That is because no one will suffer *financially* in their absence. The same can be said about a retiree, so long as the retirement savings is sufficient in size and is protected from other risks, like long-term care, liability, inflation, and estate taxes.

If life insurance replaces a working person's income should they die prior to retirement, how does one calculate that replacement value? If you earn $80,000 per year and want to replace your entire income, what amount of money sitting in a bank or other financial institution would be required to draw $80,000 per year without spending down principal? If you draw 5% from the account each year, it would require $1,600,000 in an account to provide $80,000 annually. If you don't have an account that size, life insurance can make up the difference in your absence so that your family can continue their lifestyle even after you are gone.

There are lots of kinds of life insurance, but the two basic types are either term or permanent policies.

Like the name implies, term insurance is designed to be temporary. If you are 35 years old and want to have life insurance until you are ready to retire at 65, you may want to explore a 30-year term policy. If you die before you retire, your family gets the lump-sum death benefit, puts it in a financial account, and can continue to draw your salary. If you live to 65, the term insurance expires, and you will need to rely on your retirement savings and investments to keep your income coming each year.

Permanent insurance differs from term insurance in that it is designed to pay a claim when you die, regardless of your age. There are a large number of different types of products on the market, and new products are being introduced all the time. I will do my best to summarize the main types here, but I urge you to make sure you thoroughly understand a life insurance product before buying it.

The main types of permanent life insurance are as follows:

- Whole Life
- Universal Life
- Variable Life
- Variable Universal Life

While there are other hybrid contracts, some of which are linked to returns of an equity index or to ancillary long-term care benefits, these are the primary four. I will aim to describe each one, including the uses and pros and cons of each, as well as a brief history of how the products were developed to give them some context.

Whole Life: The concept of whole life insurance has been around for ages. At one time, it was the only alternative to term insurance. Most of the policies were issued by mutual life insurance companies—those that were owned by the policyholders and had no external stockholders at all. Mutual companies are owned by, and for the exclusive benefit of, their policyholders, and they typically pay dividends on their whole life policies based on the underlying performance of the company's general accounts.

With whole life insurance, just about every feature of the policy is guaranteed contractually—the premium, the cash value schedule, and the death benefit. The dividends, if any, are not guaranteed, but the top carriers have had a strong history of paying them. Today, there are very few mutual insurance companies left, which means very little choice in the whole life marketplace. Many companies have "demutualized," which means that they went public and allowed stockholders to own the company instead of policyholders. In these cases, policyholders were given some stock based on their policy ownership, but in my opinion, this process never worked out well for the policyholders. Now, when the companies pay dividends, they have to think about the stockholders before their policyholders, and that wouldn't make me happy as a policyholder! The good news is that there are still a few very strong mutual companies writing high quality whole life insurance policies.

Because whole life has built-in guarantees on most features, it is the most expensive life insurance policy one can buy in terms of the annual premium. However, it also can be designed to grow cash values and can be a "permission slip" to spend other assets down, knowing that heirs (or surviving spouses or partners) will receive a predictable death benefit.

Whole life can be structured to have premiums paid for life or for a specific number of years, as long as that number is at least seven. Life insurance bought with premiums for fewer than seven years has a special place in the tax code that is not favorable, being dubbed a "modified endowment contract" instead of "life insurance" by the IRS. There are other cases in which that can occur as well, and if you want the cash value to build-up in a tax-deferred and potentially income tax-free way in the policies, it is critical to make sure when you buy one that it is not a modified endowment contract.

On a personal level, I own significant whole life insurance and have used the cash values over the years in a number of ways—as a down payment on my first home, as start-up capital when I opened Brotman Financial Group, and as working capital for my family on a number of occasions. I always replace the cash values to keep the contracts growing, as I believe they represent a cornerstone of my family's financial well-being and wealth building efforts. Used properly, whole life insurance can be a meaningful asset class in a portfolio and a useful cash equivalent with more unique tax advantages than any other financial product.

Universal Life: For decades, whole life insurance was the core product of the insurance industry. Then, in the 1980s, interest rates in the U.S. were so high that whole life was perceived by some as noncompetitive relative to banking products like certificates of deposit. In a reactive way, and nearly in a panic over losing market share to banks, universal life was born.

With universal life, the growth in the policies became interest rate sensitive. The death benefits were still guaranteed, but the premiums were not. So, if interest rates went up or stayed high, policies built more cash, whereas if interest rates dropped the policies would not build enough cash to maintain their premium schedules, and more money would be required by policyholders to continue the policies.

This meant that some of the risk people were trying to transfer by buying life insurance, was now squarely back on the policyholders. However, in this country, we have very short memories, and therefore the belief was that interest rates would *always* stay high and that these policies were a better way to build wealth than whole life. They were often illustrated showing projections based on 12% interest rates. Needless to say, in the past 30 years, rates came down (and stayed there, as of this writing, although that won't be true forever either). These policyholders who thought they had permanent insurance with level scheduled premiums instead got premium notices many *times* higher than they expected, and many of the policies were lapsed prematurely. It was, in a word, a *disaster* for some families.

As a result of various court cases and litigation, universal life policies being issued today can have "secondary no-lapse guarantees" on them, meaning that it is now possible to get a guaranteed premium and a guaranteed death benefit and to have the cash value interest rate sensitive. These contracts now allow buyers to choose the age at which the policies will cease to be guaranteed, and the longer the guarantee, the higher the premium.

I see examples of when universal life can be an appropriate solution and recommend it frequently for estate planning, pension maximization, trust-owned insurance for estate planning or wealth replacement, and in business cases when cash value is unimportant or could be detrimental to the planning scenario. Because there is not a guaranteed cash value schedule, the premiums are much lower than those for a whole life policy. To me, universal life today is like term insurance extended for a term equal to your entire lifetime. There are very few living benefits, but from a pure cost standpoint, there is no less expensive way to guarantee a death benefit for life.

Variable Life[5]**:** Just as the 1980s meant high interest rates and the insurance companies reacted (too late to take advantage, of course) with universal life, the 1990s meant a raging bull market for equities and again the life insurance industry was afraid of losing market share—this time to the brokerage firms rather than the banks.

Variable life insurance was created to provide a way to have a self-directed investment account inside an insurance policy. The death benefit was still guaranteed, but like universal life, the premium was not guaranteed. Instead of being related to interest rates, it was related to stock market fluctuation. Again, we have short memories in this country, and again illustrations were shown reflecting 12% (or higher) annual rates of return for the underlying portfolios. Never mind the fact that the subaccounts were very expensive and that historic equity returns (net of expenses) were lower than those shown; this was the new economy where stock markets could only go up! I can still see the various financial magazine covers in my mind, reading, in essence, "Your neighbors are getting rich, why aren't you?"

Fast-forward to 2000 and the bursting of the technology stock bubble. How do you think these policies performed? In many cases, they lost nearly half their value, and as a result premiums went up a lot. Of course, if you didn't want to pay the higher premium, you could always reduce the death benefit, or surrender the policy prematurely.

I confess that the illustrations for variable life looked impressive. For very young people who wanted (as opposed to needed) the life insurance coverage, they provided a tax-favored investment vehicle with a death benefit. However, for everyone over 35 or so, instead of passing risk, they chose to bear it and to tie it to investment returns. For the majority of people who need life insurance benefits, I still don't believe that variable life is a reasonable option. To me, the safer your life insurance is, the less conservative you may need to be with your other investments, and that is a strategy that makes more sense than tying insurance benefits to the investment markets.

Variable Universal life: In this product, designed to be a hybrid between universal life and variable life, neither the death benefit, nor the premium is guaranteed. To me, this barely qualifies as life insurance anymore and is starting to look like a tax shelter with an incidental death benefit. I cannot think of a single appropriate use for this vehicle in risk management; I only see it as an investment, and that is not what life insurance is about. If you do pursue this type of insurance, make sure to fund it heavily to try to make sure you never get a surprise in your mailbox about an impending lapse.

*　　*　　*　　*　　*

As you can see, the insurance industry has created lots of different types of life insurance policies, and you have to be extremely careful when buying something designed to be permanent. Make sure you fully understand the product so you don't have any surprises 20 years down the road. Unfortunately, I see entirely too many insurance policies that were sold inappropriately to people who do not understand them. Used properly, life insurance is an amazing tool with more tax-favored treatment than any other financial vehicle. However, used improperly, it can present a major problem.

*   *   *   *   *

9. Estate Planning Documents

When people hear the term "estate planning," they generally conjure up images of very wealthy families. However, each of us has an estate made up of the property we own, however modest, and there is more to estate planning than property.

Most individuals should have four legal documents, regardless of their level of wealth or complexity of their financial or family situation:

1. Last Will and Testament
2. Durable Financial Power of Attorney
3. Living Will
4. Advanced Health Care Directive

Like many topics in this book, several volumes could be written on this subject alone. However, I'll try to give you a basic thumbnail sketch of each item so you can feel a little bit more confident approaching an attorney to assist you. Note that all four of these documents are revocable—you can destroy or modify them at any time during your lifetime, so long as you are competent to do so. Note also that I am writing this as a financial advisor and not as an attorney, and you should consult legal counsel before creating or executing any of these, or other, legal documents.

1. Last Will and Testament

The will is the only document of the four with which most people are at least somewhat familiar. We've all seen Hollywood renditions of a will reading and people around the table waiting to find out their share of their family's fortune.

However, at its core, the will is just a document to convey your property according to your wishes. It can list specific items to go to specific people (called bequests), like "my diamond engagement ring to my daughter Sally." It can also just split property among a few beneficiaries evenly (or unevenly, if you prefer).

In most cases, you may want to reference a memorandum in your will rather than listing specific bequests of tangible personal property for two reasons. First of all, it is easier to change your mind and doesn't require all new documents (or a codicil) to do so, and secondly it can reduce the likelihood that the specific property listed will require an expensive and time-consuming appraisal during the probate process for estate tax purposes.

For example, the will can simply ask the personal representative to take any attached memorandum into consideration when distributing property to heirs, and a sheet of paper can say, "I'd like my daughter, Sally, to have my engagement ring." As long as the will doesn't *require* the personal representative to give your daughter the ring, and instead *asks* the personal representative to *consider* giving her the ring, you can generally avoid an appraisal for estate tax purposes. As always, ask your attorney for specific legal advice.

When property or cash is left to minors, a trustee will need to be named (or appointed) to handle their funds for them. Personally, I have yet to meet an 18 or 21-year old mature enough to handle sudden wealth. As a result, I often suggest that documents be drafted to provide trusts for children or grandchildren until they are much older than just the age of majority in their state of residence.[6] I often see assets held for an heir's benefit, with the principal paid out in three lump sums—at ages 25, 30, and 35. For cases involving heirs who are not good with money, or who have issues with substance abuse or gambling, funds can be held in trust for life. It is also possible to skip children and leave funds directly to grandchildren, although depending on your level of wealth, this can trigger an additional federal tax—the generation-skipping transfer tax (or GSTT)—which you will need to plan carefully to avoid or minimize.

Just as importantly as dividing your property, you will use your will to name responsible parties to handle your affairs as you leave them behind as follows:

Personal Representative: This person handles the payment of your estate's debts and the collection and distribution of your property when you die. It is usually a job that lasts about nine months. It requires someone good with details, and preferably someone local to you so that they can handle courthouse visits, etc. Unless your world is very complicated, or you do not have a responsible family member local to you, it may be best to name a family member rather than your attorney, as your attorney will be generating significant fees to handle this role for your estate, and your family member will usually waive any fees that could be paid to them by the estate. You will want to name a first choice (generally your surviving spouse, if you are married) and a second choice in this role.

Guardian: This person (or people) will be asked to accept the responsibility to raise your minor children and will usually be family members. I suggest naming a single person rather than a couple, even if you are naming a sibling and his/her spouse, because in the event of a divorce between them, this can become very awkward and may require a court to render a decision before guardianship can begin. You will ideally want to name someone who has a relationship with your children already, and may prefer someone who has children of his/her own already. Again, you'll want to name a first choice and a second choice in this role, and, of course, this is an irrelevant role until both you and your spouse are deceased.

Trustee: Depending on the complexity of your estate, you may have one or many trusts created under your will. This person (or people) will be asked to accept the responsibility to handle the financial affairs for your children or other heirs and can be an advisor, a bank's trust department, or individual(s), including family member(s). It does not have to be the same person listed as the guardian for the kids. Remember that some people are great with kids but lousy with money, and vice versa. If you are fortunate enough to have a close family member who has a good relationship with your children and can manage money, he or she can absolutely play every role under your will. You'll want a first choice and a second choice in this role, and in most cases no trustee is needed until both you and your spouse are deceased.

*   *   *   *   *

2. Durable Financial Power of Attorney

While the provisions in your will do not take effect until your death, the other three legal documents will be effective only during your lifetime.

The durable financial power of attorney names the person (called your "attorney-in-fact") who can step into your shoes to make financial decisions for you if you cannot make them yourself. It could be that you are in a coma and someone needs to pay your bills, or it could be that you broke both your wrists in a car accident and cannot sign your name.

If you are married, this person is almost always your spouse. However, you can name anyone you choose. It is important to have this document at any age. Understand that this is a very powerful document, and you must have complete trust in the person you name. If you'd prefer, you can have your attorney or financial advisor hold the original document so that it can't be used until the need arises.

These documents can go into effect immediately upon being signed or can be "springing" documents, which are not useful until and unless multiple physicians attest that you are unable to make financial decisions for yourself. I strongly suggest the immediately effective documents (especially if you are married and naming your spouse) to avoid the need for a lengthy delay under duress waiting for various physicians to attest.

Like the various roles under the wills, you'll want to name a first-choice (usually your spouse) and a second choice under this document.

*   *   *   *   *

3. Living Will

4. Advanced Health Care Directive

I am going to lump the last two documents together, because many attorneys do the same thing. It is not uncommon for these documents to be a single document in "Part A and Part B" format.

Living Wills are documents in which you are naming the person who can speak freely with the physicians or hospital staff to act on your behalf. Advanced Medical Directives are the documents in which you are providing the medical community with your wishes regarding your care in the event you cannot make your own medical decisions.

The subjects covered in these documents are very morbid, but it is easier to make these decisions while you are healthy than it could be if you are later sick or incapacitated. You'll make decisions about your care if you are in a persistent vegetative state regarding pain medication, feeding, life support, and organ donation. You can also avoid adding major family drama to the traumatic experience that could be present if you become ill by having these documents drafted and giving them to the appropriate family member(s).

For married couples, the logical choice for these documents is to name the healthy spouse. You'll also want to name a back-up. I strongly suggest naming a single person to be responsible for this role so that physicians know whom to consult when treatment is being recommended. If you name your three kids simultaneously, for example, they would not only all have to be consulted, but they'd also all have to *agree* to make this a smooth process. When is the last time all of your kids agreed on seeing the same movie, much less on important life-and-death decisions?

To minimize the likelihood of conflict, name one child as your responsible party, discuss it with your kids in advance so there are no surprises or hurt feelings, and request (but do not compel) the child you named to consult with his/her siblings, if logistically possible, prior to making major decisions.

Before we leave the topic of estate planning, there are a few more items which you may want to consider in your planning:

- Have a letter of instruction or similar document left behind with detailed information about whom your heirs should call and where certain documents are in the event of an emergency or death.

- Store a list of online passwords where your family members can access them. You'll want a secure place, as it shouldn't be left on your desk at work, but one of the great difficulties for a surviving spouse or children is getting access to accounts and information if passwords are not available.

*   *   *   *   *

10.   Asset Titling

It may sound simple, but some of the biggest mistakes that families make are found simply in the way they title their possessions, particularly among married couples.

In many cases, assets are titled jointly between spouses as a matter of convenience. However, for estate tax reasons, it is often important to have significant assets in each spouse's name individually to make sure to take full advantage of certain credits allowed against potential federal or state estate taxes.

A discussion of the estate tax rules is beyond the scope of this book, but it is worth asking your financial advisor and estate planning attorney how various assets should be titled for optimal tax planning.

In addition to tax planning, there are also liability issues in titling of assets. In some states, it is important, for example, not to title an automobile in joint name because it could open up both parties (and their joint assets) to a lawsuit in the event of an accident involving either spouse behind the wheel. It is better to title an automobile to the primary driver alone, if possible, in an attempt to protect some joint property from a lawsuit.

Speaking of joint property, there are different ways to title property between two or more people, and the elections you make are critical in the planning process:

- **Joint Tenants with Rights of Survivorship (JTWROS):**

This is the most common way to title property between two or more people. It means that each owner holds an indivisible share of the property and that upon the death of one owner, the remaining owners will automatically acquire the deceased owner's share, usually equally. The challenges with JTWROS are that it doesn't allow for use of credits to protect against estate taxation, it doesn't allow property to pass under a will or to be used by the estate, and it doesn't protect the various owners from lawsuits against the other owners.

- **Joint Tenants in Entireties (TEN ENT):**

This type of property ownership is only allowed between married spouses, and is only recognized in certain states. Functionally, it is identical to JTWROS, with the exception that it provides some liability protection in the event one spouse or the other is sued. This is often the best choice for titling a personal residence shared by a married couple.

- **Joint Tenants in Common (TEN COM):**

This type of registration allows each partial owner to maintain their own personal, divisible, share of the property. The benefit is that it allows for multiple owners, even with varying percentage of ownership, and that it allows each owner to leave their share of the property under their will. It also allows for use of credits for estate tax purposes, especially if two spouses opt for this registration. However, it does not offer the liability protection, and it can put owners in a difficult position if one owner dies, leaving his or her share evenly between four children all of whom become owners of a single piece of property. If the property is liquid (i.e. a mutual fund portfolio), it isn't a big deal since shares can be identified and sold. However, if the property is a house at the beach and a few owners want to keep it while a few owners want to sell it, conflict can occur.

*   *   *   *   *

Beyond joint property, there are a number of ways to title property, either in a temporary way (for example, allowing ownership for life but not allowing control of its disposition at death), or in trust (there are countless types of trusts and other legal entities that can be established by your attorney to accomplish almost anything you'd like with your property, including skipping generations or naming charitable beneficiaries).

If you wish to by-pass the language in the will to transfer non-qualified assets directly to one or more beneficiaries, you can title an individual accounts as "Payable on Death" or "Transfer on Death," sometimes referred to as "POD" or "TOD" accounts. This will not avoid inclusion in an estate tax calculation, but it will allow accounts to be re-titled to a beneficiary more quickly upon your death. Note that there are sometimes valid reasons to *want* property to pass under the will, so it is rarely advisable to title *all* of your individual accounts as TOD.

There are some states that abide by community property laws, which means essentially that all property acquired by either spouse during the time they were married is marital property. One exception is a family inheritance going to one spouse or the other, so long as the inherited property is never re-titled jointly or comingled with community property.

Before moving on, let's discuss the impact of titling property to minors. Every state maintains their own age of majority (usually 18 or 21) and has different rules about custodial accounts. Some follow the Uniform Gifts to Minors Act (UGMA), while others follow the slightly different Uniform Transfers to Minors Act (UTMA). If an account is titled to a minor (or if a minor inherits property), it requires an adult or corporate custodian or trustee to safeguard that property for the benefit of the minor. These accounts are *irrevocable*; that is, once an account is titled to a minor, it belongs to the minor and cannot be used for other purposes.

The problems with naming minors as account owners are numerous, but the two biggest are: 1) minors are seldom ready to handle large sums of money at a young age, and 2) every dollar in a minor's name will typically reduce the amount of financial aid available for college by a dollar. As a result, titling assets directly in a minor's name is rarely, if ever, advisable.

It is better to set up trusts for minors—either under your will or by gifting to an account owned under a trust agreement. These require an attorney to draft, but can be set up to hold funds for a young person's use until they are much older than the age of majority (or even forever), and won't impact financial aid as adversely.

Some college planning accounts allow minors to be named as *beneficiaries*, as opposed to owners, and that can have multiple benefits—a better financial aid outcome, the ability for parents or grandparents to direct the funds to a college (or even to change the beneficiary on an account)—while still keeping it outside of the parents' or grandparents' estates for tax purposes.

We have only scratched the surface on asset titling in this brief section. The titling of assets is critical and complicated enough that I recommend getting assistance from your financial advisor and attorney as a part of your overall planning. It can be a cumbersome process to re-title property, but it is rarely expensive and is much easier to accomplish while everyone is alive and competent, as opposed to after someone dies or becomes incapacitated.

* * * * *

11. Beneficiary Designations

When completing your contingency planning, in addition to titling your assets properly, you will also want to name beneficiaries on various accounts and insurance policies very carefully. That is because the beneficiary designation on an account or insurance policy supersedes anything listed in the will.

If your will says that you want your three children to share equally in your assets, but your IRA names only your oldest child (or your ex-wife, or anyone else), only the person or people named on the beneficiary designation can inherit that property **no matter what the will states**.

There are lots of considerations when making beneficiary elections, some of which are state-specific, so this chapter can only provide a cursory review of those decisions. You'll want to talk with your attorney, financial advisor, and insurance agent to make sure the elections you make are appropriate in your situation.

If you intend your will to have trust provisions to hold assets for your children until specific ages, you need to make sure that property actually passes under the will to fund that trust. We often see life insurance proceeds designated that way. The primary beneficiary may be your spouse and the contingent beneficiary may read: "Trustee(s) under the Last Will and Testament of the Insured." This makes sure that the trust is funded, and also has other potential estate planning benefits including the utilization of various tax credits and liquidity for the estate.

Qualified retirement plans and IRAs are eligible for special tax treatment if they are paid directly to named beneficiaries (or to trusts with very specific language relating to the accounts). These provisions are called "stretch" provisions. When a spouse is the named beneficiary of a qualified account, he or she can deposit those assets directly into his or her own IRA account and can generally use them with the same rules as their own plan. There are lots of exceptions to this rule dealing with one spouse over age 70 ½ and one under that age, and spouses with significant age differences between them, etc. You'll want to consult your tax advisor or CPA prior to making elections under these plans.

For beneficiaries other than spouses on qualified plan accounts or IRAs, the stretch provisions allow a beneficiary to fund a "beneficiary distribution account" (or IRA-BDA) and to take distributions annually, starting at whatever age they are currently, based on their life expectancy. That means that a 20-year old beneficiary only has to make a small required distribution each year. This has a very positive long-term impact on the account balance and the tax-deferral, and heirs will want to use these BDA accounts wisely and opportunistically, with the help of their financial and tax advisors.

One more thought on this brief description of beneficiary naming. You can designate beneficiaries to receive a percentage of an account either *"per capita"* ("by head") or *"per stirpes"* ("by root"), and the difference is very significant.

Let's say you have three children, and each of your children has two children of their own. If you name your children as your beneficiaries equally on an account, and they are all living when you die, they will each get 1/3 of the account balance. However, if one of your children predeceases you, those two Latin words become very important. In a *per capita* arrangement, distribution is split evenly only among your living beneficiaries. So, your assets would be split only between your two living children at the time 50/50. This would potentially disinherit two of your grandchildren by accident! If you name your kids under a *per stirpes* arrangement, your two living children in this example would still get 1/3 each, but your two grandchildren of your deceased child would split that child's 1/3 share equally. In this scenario, your family would share "by root" rather than "by head," so no one would accidentally be disinherited.

*   *   *   *   *

As with all advice in this book, in keeping with the fact that "one size never fits all," you'll want to consult your financial, tax, and legal advisors to discuss the details of these risk management strategies, products, and solutions, to determine which are most appropriate for your situation.

Next, we turn our attention to cash flow.

CHAPTER FIVE

PAY YOURSELF FIRST

THE MOST IMPORTANT BILL TO PAY EVERY MONTH

Now that we have addressed the financial planning process and handled the contingency planning, let's turn our attention in the last few chapters to the manner in which you save, invest, and ideally grow your net worth until you reach financial independence.

On the surface, saving money sounds like a straight-forward proposition. If you spend less than you make, you are saving money. But if it were really that easy, wouldn't we all be better at it naturally?

What many households do from month-to-month is bring in the income, pay the bills, and hope that something is left over on the last day of the month. If you are in one of the households employing this strategy and you have money left at the end of the month (at least *most* of the time), that is an excellent start—you are living within your means. However, allow me the leeway to also suggest that someone is not necessarily a great saver simply because there is money left over at the end of the month in a checking account.

The strategy I would like to describe to you is one which I call "Pay Yourself First." The concept is simple. Each month, you put away your allocation for savings or investment first (before you pay any bills). Then, you adjust your lifestyle (or budget) as if the money you saved was never earned in the first place.

Of all the checks you write every month, the one that is most important might be the one that you write to yourself. If you are free of adverse debt and have built your emergency fund to three-six months expenses or more (per our discussion in Chapter Three), the next step towards wealth building and financial independence, is to build your asset base. This can take several forms—let's call them Phase 1 and Phase 2 of savings.

In Phase 1 of savings, you set an objective to save a specific percentage of your gross income each month. At our firm, we set an initial target of 15% for our clients, but you can start with any percentage, just to get the process underway. If your household's gross income is $10,000 per month, the Phase 1 objective will be to save $1,500 per month (15%). If, due to cash flow considerations, you feel the need to set an intermediate goal of less than 15% (say $750) to get started, it is an excellent step in the process, because it helps you to create good habits.

In the example above, saving 15% of gross income means setting a spending limit at $8,500 a month, even though you are earning $10,000. If you can live on the $8,500 per month, you'll be able to save the $1,500 each month comfortably and won't miss it. We'll discuss in the next chapter where to put the $1,500 each month, but for now, let's at least agree that it won't be used for personal spending or household bills.

Phase 2 of savings occurs after you have reached the 15% objective, are living within 85% of your means, have maintained your emergency fund, and have remained free of adverse debt. This phase involves setting a long-term goal and creating metrics to measure your progress along the way.

If your goal is to retire in twenty years, for example, it is possible to estimate how much money you'll need to save or invest every month from now until retirement to help you reach your goal. Through the power of compounding interest and dollar-cost averaging, you can actually build quite a large potential nest egg by paying yourself first every month and checking your progress regularly. If you check your progress every 6-12 months, you can adjust the amount you're saving or investing each month as needed to stay on track.

Let me provide an example of the power of compounding interest and dollar-cost averaging[7]:

If you were to put away $2,000 per month for 20 years (240 months), the total nominal amount of money that you would have saved or invested would be $480,000 ($2,000 x 240 months). However, if the funds were in an account which experienced a 7% annualized rate of return, your account will have grown to $1,052,764. (Note that assuming a 7% return on capital, while historically reasonable, has been very challenging for the first decade plus of the 21st century. Note also that the impact of taxes is not being considered in this example.)

Imagine the power of setting aside 15% or more of your income and earning a reasonable rate of return for many years. The really important factor is to have time on your side. If you are in your 20s, 30s, or 40s and want to start saving for retirement, you have several decades to watch your accounts grow and to reach for a lofty retirement goal. For people closer to retirement, it is much harder to reach the target in fewer years. I don't say that to discourage getting started saving and investing at any age, but I want specifically to encourage young people to save regularly from as early an age as possible. Saving early and routinely, staying free of adverse debt, and paying yourself first, are major determinants of financial independence, and will help you be on your way to reaching your goals.

If you need assistance with the calculation, there are tools online to calculate retirement needs, or you can enlist the assistance of a financial advisor. You or your planner can create various hypothetical illustrations to build a plan and monitor it regularly. Assumptions on rates of return and inflation, along with your ability to save and invest money regularly, will help you determine how soon you may be able to reach your goal. Once you have eliminated adverse debt and paid yourself first with 15% of your income each month, it will be time to get serious about creating a savings and investment plan, which we will discuss in the next chapter.

CHAPTER SIX

INVESTING BASICS

SIX DECISIONS YOU NEED TO MAKE BEFORE YOU START INVESTING

More often than not, when people call our office for a consultation, the first statement they make starts with something along the lines of "I/We have a portfolio that . . ." It seems that the desire to allocate, rebalance, or somehow optimize a portfolio is on the top of everyone's mind. Even before we talk about investment choices, asset classes, manager selection, etc., there are important decisions that each investor needs to make. In this chapter, we will discuss six of the major decisions that need to be made prior to opening your first account:

1) Risks Associated with Investing
2) Costs Inherent in Investing
3) Hiring Portfolio Managers vs. Doing it Yourself
4) Qualified vs. Non-Qualified Accounts
5) Active vs. Passive Portfolio Management
6) Strategic vs. Tactical Portfolio Management

I will attempt to cover each of these topics in the context of a rational fact base, along with the philosophical theories and emotional responses inherent in the investing experience.

1) Risks Associated with Investing

No conversation about investing can begin without first discussing the risks involved. Lawyers have written 200+ page prospectuses on the subject in the name of consumer protection, but I have yet to meet a client who has actually read one in its entirety. Thus, this will aim to over-simplify the issues just to get you thinking about them. It is not designed to replace the prospectus you receive (and allegedly read and understand) every time you make an investment.

During the data gathering process in Chapter Two, we discussed a part of the initial questionnaire that is dedicated to determining your risk tolerance as an investor. These questionnaires are absolutely inadequate to assess fully the risk tolerance of a client, and in fact can be problematic because the responses are often biased by recent experiences. If a questionnaire is completed after a good year in the markets, responses are likely to be overly optimistic and reflect a more aggressive tolerance than may be accurate, whereas if a questionnaire is completed after a bad year in the markets, responses are likely to be overly pessimistic and reflect conservatism far exceeding an "appropriate" response level.

In addition to the challenges with self-reporting one's own risk tolerance, there is also the fact that couples and partners often don't agree on risk levels.

One spouse may be more skittish, while the other is more of a daredevil. Care must be taken to make sure each spouse or partner is comfortable in a planning engagement, by treating each account differently based upon its owner of record, stated purpose, and time horizon.

Lastly, when people think about investment risk, they almost always focus only on the "market risk"— the possibility that an account value can go down. There are other risks we need to be concerned about, depending on the holdings in a portfolio. In addition to market risk, there are also the following:

- **Interest-rate risk:**

With certain securities or portfolios, one of the greatest risks is that interest rates will move in a direction adverse to the underlying holdings. If, for example, a portfolio holds nothing but long-term bonds, and interest rates rise, the market value of those bonds will likely drop precipitously. In another example, if the account holds long-term certificates of deposit at 1.5%, and interest rates rise to 6%, the account holder would either have to sell at an adverse price, pay a penalty for early withdrawal, or potentially miss out on the opportunity of earning a higher return on his or her funds. Thus, the movements of interest rates can impact not only the value of a portfolio, but can also create opportunity costs by missing better interest-rate opportunities.

- ## Inflation/Purchasing power risk:

While market risk and interest risk are somewhat easy to understand, the risks associated with inflation are much more subtle. Inflation adjusts the value of a currency by creating a higher nominal cost for goods and services. For an example of inflation, consider the postage stamp. As recently as the early 1970s, the cost to mail a letter with the U.S. Postal Service was $0.06. As of this writing, some 40 years later, the cost to mail the same letter is $0.46. That means that the cost of a single stamp is nearly **eight times** higher than it was only 40 years ago. Inflation impacts all goods and services, but does so unequally. That means the cost of housing, automobiles, education, groceries, leisure, and basically anything you can name will be more expensive in the future than today, and by an uncertain amount. Consider also that retirement could be a 30-40 year period of time, and it is clear that inflation will play a major role in determining more or less successful retirement planning outcomes.

If a security or portfolio is providing a return greater than the rate of inflation, it is said to be providing a positive inflation-adjusted return. On the other hand, if the security or portfolio is providing a return that is negative, or that is positive but less than inflation, it is said to have a negative inflation-adjusted return.

Keeping ahead of inflation protects an investor's purchasing power, and failing to do so subsequently erodes purchasing power so that even an account balance that is "higher" from one year to the next might provide a lifestyle that is "lower" than in prior years.

- **Currency/Exchange rate risk:**

A typical portfolio is likely to contain securities issued over the world, not just in the United States. As such, one of the risks in investing is the impact that constantly-changing exchange rates between currencies play on a portfolio. If you have a portfolio denominated in the U.S. dollar, but some of your securities are denominated in the Japanese yen, a movement of the number of yen equivalent to each dollar will impact your portfolio returns.

Note that we aren't just talking about the risk that a security's price is impacted by a currency exchange-rate adjustment due to its denomination, but also the risk that the financial results (profit or loss) of the company issuing the underlying security is impacted by an exchange rate adjustment. The stock you own in a company in North Carolina, which does significant business in Germany, could be impacted by the exchange rate between the dollar and the euro, even though it is a domestic (U.S.) stock in your portfolio.

- **Political/Legislative/Taxation risk:**

For the purposes of this brief summary, I lumped together the risks created by politics, legislation, and taxation, both domestically and internationally, even though they are each distinct.

International relations can impact a portfolio in lots of ways—by impacting the exchange rate, by seeing trade imbalances, tariffs imposed, or embargos applied. As we know all too well, even politics in Washington can impact our portfolios, mostly because investors on a macro level prefer certainty to uncertainty, and there has been a lot of political uncertainty over the past decade or so as of this writing.

From a legislative standpoint, much of the uncertainty overlaps into the realm of taxation, and a simple change by Congress on the way a dividend, interest payment, or capital gain will be taxed can send shockwaves through an equity or bond market, just like a change to deductibility of mortgage interest would impact the real estate markets dramatically.

- **Liquidity/Marketability risk:**

In addition to the macro-level risks discussed above, there is a risk on a more micro-level to an investor holding securities that have limited liquidity or marketability. In other words, if a security cannot readily be sold, either due to a restriction or covenant, or due to the fact that there is simply not a willing buyer, it may impact the market price of that security adversely.

As an example, think of your home. In a so-called "sellers' market" there are more buyers than homes for sale and, therefore, houses are readily marketable and prices go up. On the other hand, in a so-called "buyers' market," there are more homes for sale than willing buyers and, therefore, houses are difficult to sell (have limited marketability) and prices go down.

*   *   *   *   *

Beyond all of the risks we've discussed is perhaps the biggest risk of all—**behavioral risk**—the natural tendency we all have to act on our emotions, causing us to do exactly the wrong thing at exactly the wrong time. Sometimes, it is based on the knee-jerk reaction to sell near the bottom of a market cycle because you "just can't take any more of a loss" or to buy near the top of a market cycle because you "don't want to miss out on such a great opportunity to make money."

Behavioral risk also brings out our own personal biases—on a variety of issues. For example, *proximity bias* is the tendency for investors to overweight their portfolios towards securities domiciled in their country of residence. In the U.S., that might mean holding 80 or 90 percent of a portfolio in American securities, even though the U.S. equity markets make up only about 50 percent of the world's market capitalization.

There is also a *familiarity bias* which can lead investors only to choose securities familiar to them. While household names can be a fine way to select certain services or products, it may not be the best way to pick stocks. In fact, in some cases, the big name companies who put their names on the football or baseball stadium in your hometown may actually be illustrating a terrible habit of overspending, instead of good fiscal management. Buying names you know is also not the same for an amateur investor and a seasoned one. It may be better to rely on professional advice or research, as opposed to just your name brand recognition when making an investment.

Needless to say, we are our own worst enemies when it comes to our emotional reactions and personal biases, and that is why I suggest that even financial advisors use an objective and unrelated financial advisor themselves. I rely on a study group with six other advisors in it, and my relationship with them is invaluable to me, personally, professionally, and financially.

It is important to use the contingency planning process to provide some relief from various types of financial risks and to control those risks that can be controlled. For those that can't be controlled, people need to rely on their advisors to help lead them through volatile times dispassionately, and to avoid becoming victims of the behavioral risks resident in each of us.

*　　*　　*　　*　　*

2) Costs Inherent in Investing

Like any product or service, investment management has various costs. Some of those costs are readily apparent on a statement (sometimes called "fee transparency"), while others are embedded in various products in the form of fees, commissions, or "expense ratios."

If you elect the *do it yourself* approach, the costs will be limited to your custodian(s) and your asset manager(s), both of which will be defined below. If you use advisor(s) of some kind—a financial advisor, stock broker, insurance agent, banker, etc., you will also have a cost for their involvement.

Expense ratios are the underlying costs in a mutual fund or exchange-traded fund. These are not reflected on your statement, but their impact cannot be ignored. That is because the returns you experience owning mutual funds are reported to you *net* of those underlying expenses. All funds have some cost to them—some are very modest (a passively-managed domestic equity fund might cost 0.10%-0.25% per year)—while some are very expensive (actively managed international equity funds can cost 2.25% per year or more).

In a retail mutual fund, often called an "A," a "B," or a "C" share, your advisor and broker/dealer are paid either a commission to buy the fund, a portion of the fund expense ratio, or both. In "institutional" or "no load" funds, your advisor and broker/dealer are not paid a commission or a portion of the expense ratio, and instead will impose a portfolio services fee (usually a percentage of the assets in the account) transparently on your statement or a retainer fee (usually a flat annual fee in lieu of or in addition to the portfolio services fee) by separate invoice.

Your custodian is the holder of your actual accounts themselves—and has "custody" of your cash, stocks, bonds, funds, or other holdings. Some large brokerage firms are "self-clearing," which means that they are their own clearing firm. For independent advisors, or those affiliated with small broker/dealers, banks, or insurance companies, there is usually a 3rd-party custodian. As we discussed earlier in the book, the most common in the U.S. are National Financial Services, Schwab, and Pershing. You will find language on your statement to help you determine who your custodian is, and any deposits made to an account are typically made payable to the custodian directly.

Custodians are paid in several ways—annual account fees, trading and transaction fees, alternative asset custody fees, and check-writing or debit card access fees, to name a few. Some also have fees imposed for account inactivity or for accounts below a certain market value. These fees are transparent on your statement. Your advisor does not share in these fees, and in fact pays them also if he/she maintains personal accounts with the same custodian.

Your advisor may manage your accounts personally or may use an institutional third-party money manager to manage them. If a third-party is used, the account fees tend to be higher as there is another party in the mix. That is not to suggest that using a third-party is a bad idea—for larger accounts (over $200,000 or so), price breaks can be significant and trading costs and custody fees are often included, so the cost difference can be modest. For smaller accounts (under $200,000 or so) a third-party manager can be prohibitively expensive and may be unnecessary.

As we discussed in Chapter Two, financial advisors have many different models on how to charge for their planning services. However, from an asset management standpoint, it is common to see advisory fees between 1.0% and 2.5% per year, depending on the firm you use, your level of assets being managed, and the level of service you need or want.

Brokerage firms (broker/dealers) are those organizations that trade securities for their own accounts or on behalf of their account-holders. They are usually paid a portion of the advisory fee, so that the all-in advisory fee on a managed account includes the advisor, the broker/dealer, and possibly the custodian and/or third-party manager. Basically everything is covered in a portfolio services fee except some transaction costs, account-level custody costs, and the expense ratios of underlying funds.

As a firm, we consider our value proposition to be based on financial planning advice, client service, and other factors not strictly tied to asset management. I suspect that many independent financial advisors feel exactly the same way. Our firm uses a model in which we charge a fee on assets (and/or a retainer fee for clients with less than our current account minimum under management) which covers our ongoing comprehensive financial planning services. Therefore, the fee charged to the accounts is not solely for investment management, but also covers the ongoing monitoring of our clients' financial plans.

For the sake of example, at the time of this printing, our firm charges 1.1% as an asset management fee for third-party managed accounts (which is roughly 1.0% to our firm and 0.1% to our broker/dealer) and 1.35% for discretionary accounts managed by our firm directly (which is roughly 1.2% to our firm and 0.15% to our broker/dealer). Note that as the assets under management for a single client get larger our asset management fees get reduced, generally at $3,000,000 and again at $10,000,000.

Needless to say, costs will have an impact on investment performance. In order to net a 6% return after expenses, an average return closer to 8% would be required by the fund managers. Remember that in a retail share, returns are reported net of expenses, whereas in an institutional share, returns are reported net of only the expense ratio. In plain English, that means that account holders are paying for assets to be managed, whether those fees appear transparently on their statements or not. The key number to a client is always going to be the total return net of expenses and fees earned by the account.

For most investors, the question is "Can my financial advisor provide enough value, advice, and behavior management to cover his or her expenses?" At the same time, from purely an asset management standpoint, we can ask, "Can my financial advisor do better with 98% of my money than I can do with 99% of my money?" If the answer to either question is yes, your advisor is at least covering his or her costs. If not, there may still be other value in working with an advisor—time savings, family communication, and other intangibles—that make it worthwhile.

Ultimately, it is up to the client to determine if there is *value* in the relationship. The value is often derived when something goes wrong in a family's situation and the contingency planning has to be activated. I think it has been said that any captain can navigate in calm seas; the captain you want with you is the one who can navigate in choppy seas.

*   *   *   *   *

3) Hiring Portfolio Managers vs. Doing it Yourself

With all of the research tools available online today and the easy access to accounts, there is no reason why you can't just do this yourself. However, the fact that Home Depot will allow me to buy the supplies to build my own house does not qualify me as a homebuilder.

For individuals with the time, talent, and inclination to put together their own portfolios, a wealth of information is available to make that possible. I would argue, of course, that not everyone should attempt to do this on their own.

There are lots of rational reasons why this is so: people are too busy to be watching markets, there is so much information that it is hard to differentiate the nuggets of wisdom from the noise, and the investment options have continued to get more complicated and require an enormous amount of study just to stay abreast of them all.

As compelling as some of those reasons can be, allow me to suggest that the primary benefit to working with a financial advisor is not a rational one, but an emotional one. Maintaining financial discipline is not unlike maintaining a personal fitness discipline. We can all buy a treadmill and put it in our basement, but not all of us will use it regularly, if at all, and even those of us who use it may not use it *correctly.* Thus, by hiring a personal trainer, we can stay on track, motivated, and accountable, and I believe that results are generally better that way.

While people have been trained by our 24-hour financial media to "Don't just sit there—do something," in the financial planning space sometimes the best advice we can give to a client with a well-designed portfolio is to *do nothing.* When markets are volatile and the media is signaling the end of the world as we know it, *do nothing differently—stay the course.* When the tech stocks are raging and neighbors are bragging about getting rich quickly, *do nothing differently— stay the course.* When real estate speculators are flipping houses and making quick profits, *do nothing differently—stay the course.* If this sounds a little boring, it can be. However, if you have set a course for financial independence, it is the emotional reaction to external events that is most likely to derail you. So just like an extra 10 minutes on the treadmill might sound tedious, doing it will produce results. Some people made a lot of money on tech stocks or flipping houses;

others lost their entire nest eggs in early 2000 or are still stuck with real estate that they can't sell, even at a big loss. That isn't investing, it is gambling. If you find gambling entertaining, may I suggest that a trip to Las Vegas will be more fun than watching CNBC and picking stocks?

The only reason that your planning should change dramatically is because something major has happened in your *life*. That is when an advisor becomes a sounding board, a confidant, and a co-pilot. My ability to build portfolios might be better than yours, or it might not. But my ability to help you maintain the discipline to stay the course in the face of challenging circumstances or external noise could be *priceless*.

For people who made dramatic portfolio changes in November 2008 believing that the world was in-fact ending, they may never recover. For people who stopped paying themselves first and making regular contributions to their investment accounts, their recovery has been long and slow. But for those who kept paying themselves first and maintained their laser-like focus on their goals and not on the evening news' crisis du jour, they have come out ahead. It wasn't without some uncomfortable moments—like the personal training mantra would suggest, sometimes no pain means no gain. But the only thing we can control is our *behavior*, not the stimuli that make us think we have to *do something* all the time.

The benefit to solid objective advice is often related to your family, your life, and your emotions, more than to technical market metrics.

While it is true that a few people have the discipline to get a workout every day and to do it properly without a personal trainer, it is my fervent belief that only a small percentage of people should even attempt to do financial planning alone.

* * * * *

4) Qualified vs. Non-Qualified Accounts

In the next chapter, we will be concentrating on the types of asset classes often included in a portfolio. However, it is first important to discuss the various types of accounts that can be established (which are mutually exclusive from the actual underlying holdings).

For our purposes, there are two primary types of accounts to consider for savings and investment: qualified and non-qualified accounts.

While there are many variations that are somewhat beyond the scope of this book, for our purposes, we'll call any type of retirement plan or account a "qualified" account. That means 401(k) plans, 403(b) tax-sheltered annuities, individual retirement accounts (IRAs), SEP IRAs, SIMPLE IRAs, and other retirement vehicles will be considered "qualified" for our limited purposes moving forward.

Note that the definition of a "qualified retirement plan" has to do with the IRS determination that an employer-sponsored plan meets all of the necessary criteria to receive favorable income tax treatment. Note also that IRAs in their various forms are not "qualified retirement plans" by definition, but will be grouped with "qualified accounts" for our purposes in this book. In addition the Roth IRA, which is a type of IRA, and the Roth 401(k), which is a type of employer-sponsored retirement plan, both with very distinct tax properties, will also be considered "qualified" for our limited purposes here, since they have similar age restrictions to other types of IRAs and retirement plans.

Qualified accounts are designed for long-term, retirement savings. With a few exceptions, they tend to have very significant penalties for withdrawals prior to age 59 ½, and should be considered long-term money that is unavailable for any purpose other than retirement. Sometimes an employer will fund these accounts for an employee, while other times the employee will make his or her own contributions. In a third scenario, there are lots of plans in which both the employer and the employee are making contributions for the employee's benefit.

If your employer is making contributions on your behalf, there is usually a "vesting schedule" which states that if your employment ends before a certain number of years have passed (often 5-7 years), you will not be able to take all of the funds the employer contributed on your behalf with you when you go. All contributions that you have made to a plan will be 100% vested to you immediately, and you'll be able to take those funds with you at any time you leave an employer. Remember that even when leaving an employer, any qualified accounts will still be subject to penalties and fees if you withdraw the funds prematurely. You can move funds from one plan to another (sometimes called a "rollover" and sometimes called a "trustee-to-trustee transfer," depending on the type of account being closed and the specific type of account receiving the funds) without a fee, tax, or penalty under most circumstances.

The second general type of account to consider is a "non-qualified" account, which for our purposes will include brokerage accounts, mutual fund accounts, deferred compensation plans, employee stock purchase plans, common stock dividend reinvestment programs, and for the remainder of this book, any account that is not defined as a "qualified" account.

Non-qualified accounts are very flexible and can usually allow for some liquidity should funds be needed earlier than originally anticipated. These accounts historically have received a more favorable "capital gains" tax treatment, so long as assets are held more than one year, and they are accessible to you almost anytime.

The reason for this distinction is that there is a vast difference in the way qualified and non-qualified accounts are treated, not only from a tax perspective, but also from a liquidity perspective.

Once you have funded your cash emergency fund, it will be time to start funding qualified and/or non-qualified accounts as well.

When you are first getting started with any of these types of vehicles, the major considerations for you to consider are the following:

- **Your current tax bracket:**

The higher your tax bill, the more likely you are to benefit from making the maximum contributions possible to a qualified retirement plan. If your tax bracket is lower, either the Roth IRA or Roth 401(k) may provide a good mechanism for tax-deferred savings, without the tax deduction up front.

- **Your likely tax bracket in retirement:**

Knowing that tax rates and rules change constantly and that none of us has a crystal ball, this can be tough. However, having a sense of your current income versus your future income and net worth will help determine which type of account to use. If your future income is likely to be similar or higher than your present income, a Roth IRA or Roth 401(k) may be more favorable than traditional IRAs or qualified plans. If you are likely to have less income in your retirement years than you do today, the reverse is true. In that case, you will likely benefit more from the up-front tax deduction that a traditional IRA or retirement plan allows.

- **Your potential need for liquidity:**

If there is a possibility that some of your funds might be needed before age 59 ½, it is important to have them in non-qualified accounts where assets can generally be sold and the proceeds can be reached with minimal fees, penalties, etc . . . .

- **The availability of an employer contribution and whether it is contingent on you making a contribution yourself (i.e. a matching contribution on a 401(k) or 403(b)):**

In a perfect world, you would be in a position to make a maximum contribution to your retirement (qualified) plan, to receive a matching contribution or profit-sharing contribution of some kind from your employer, and also to be able to make a meaningful contribution to a non-qualified account.

As most families do not reside in a perfect world, the place to start might be making enough of a contribution to an employer-sponsored retirement plan in order to maximize the matching contribution. In other words, if your employer's qualified plan will match fifty cents for every dollar that you contribute up to 6% of your salary, that means that if you put away 6%, they will put away an additional 3% of your salary into the plan for you. That is like a tax-deferred raise, and assuming you stay with your employer long enough to vest in the matching contributions, it can make a big difference to your retirement income. In addition, if you set a minimum target for your savings rate at 15% and your employer is putting in 3%, you only need to come up with 12% of your gross income to move from Phase 1 to Phase 2, as discussed in Chapter Five.

Using that same example, you are now putting away six percent to your qualified account and your employer is putting in another three percent, so where does the rest of your monthly savings go? If you are in a high income tax bracket, you may want to put more than six percent into the qualified plan until you reach your maximum allowable limit, after which funds can go into a non-qualified account. If you are not in a very high tax bracket, you might benefit more by depositing your additional monthly savings into a non-qualified account (after taking full advantage of your employer's maximum matching contribution).

This was an over-simplified conversation on qualified versus non-qualified accounts, but hopefully it highlighted a few of the thought processes required to make an important decision regarding what type of account(s) to fund once you start saving and investing.

*   *   *   *   *

5) Active vs. Passive Portfolio Management

The active versus passive debate is one that has raged for decades and is likely to continue for decades more. Allow me to describe the two strategies a bit so you can understand the important differences between them.

Active management is a portfolio or fund manager's attempt to *beat* a market or index, aiming to use allegedly superior skills or research capabilities in selecting securities, timing market movements, and identifying hidden opportunities or anomalies in the investing universe.

With active management, trading will often be frequent as the portfolio turns over holdings regularly, resulting in higher costs and taxes, but the premise is that the managers are skillful enough to offset costs and taxes with excess investment returns and are therefore worth the extra expense.

Passive management is the use of a portfolio that aims to participate in the returns of various indices or markets, but makes no attempt to trade actively or to *beat* or *time* a market. Costs and taxes tend to be much lower, and in a nutshell, this strategy presumes that markets are efficient and cannot be timed or beaten with any degree of consistency, and that it is better to own the market entirely. In a sense, it is an "if you can't beat them, join them" mentality.

With passive management, assets will be allocated in a fund or portfolio and left alone; a buy and hold approach. Sometimes passive managers will link their holdings to an index (appropriately called index funds), whereas sometimes they will employ a buy-and-hold approach without using a direct index link. Thus, even with a passive manager, an investor may not have to accept a return equal to an index (on the upside or the downside of the market); there may still be opportunity for a manager to use a buy-and-hold strategy with an overlay of criteria to determine *which securities* to buy-and-hold.

Volumes have been written on this debate opining on why one approach is somehow conclusively superior to the other. All of the arguments are lucid, but I'd like to weigh in with my own philosophy on the subject.

First, I believe that markets are efficient—that is, that they take all available information into consideration when securities are priced. As a result, few (if any) arbitrage opportunities or anomalies are available to investors, and therefore it is very unlikely that a manager will uncover a security which is *mistakenly* underpriced.

Second, the fact that most active managers *trail* their benchmarks in any given year leads me to believe that active management in most cases is not worth the higher expenses. Betting on a small number of managers to select a finite number of securities, to buy just the right thing at just the right time, and then to sell just the right thing at just the right time, feels like a more speculative approach than owning the markets entirely. It also can't be done with any regularity. Remember that when one active manager is *buying* ABC stock, another one must be *selling* ABC stock. One of them must be wrong about the immediate future of the stock price, no? And, if you happen to own two active funds and one is buying ABC while the other is selling ABC, it isn't a break-even for you. As a shareholder of each fund, you pay trading costs twice, taxes on any gains on the sale, and your effective "loss" is equal to two trading charges and any taxes due.

Third, in my opinion, passive management should not be constrained to link to a specific index. With apologies to John Bogle, the founder of Vanguard and arguably the father of passive investing, I am only partly in his camp. I do believe that costs matter and that taxes matter and that a passive strategy with the right diversification among asset classes makes more sense than trying to pick winners. *(Note: We will discuss diversification and portfolio design in greater detail in Chapter Seven).* However, I do not like pure index funds very much, as they have a tragic flaw underneath the wrapper of low costs and market-matching returns. The problem with an index fund is that it is forced to buy securities or to sell securities without any flexibility at all.

Using the S&P 500 Index[8] as an example, when Standard & Poor's announces that XYZ stock is joining the index, many investors buy up the shares of stock in anticipation of the company joining the index funds. This buying increases the stock price, *before* an index fund can accumulate enough shares to keep its market index weighting. That means that an index fund often pays an artificially *high* price for securities it buys.

Likewise, when Standard & Poor's announces that XYZ stock is *leaving* the index, many investors sell the shares of stock in anticipation of the company leaving the index funds. This selling decreases the stock price, *before* an index fund can divest itself of all of its shares. That means that an index fund often receives an artificially *low* price for securities it sells.

Lastly, while passive management (without purely indexing) makes more sense to me as a core strategy than active management, it is not a panacea. I do believe that as a "satellite" strategy it is fine to use some active management in a portfolio, especially in the fixed income securities markets.

*   *   *   *   *

6) Strategic vs. Tactical Portfolio Management

Similar to the discussion on active and passive investment management is the discussion on strategic vs. tactical management.

Strategic money management utilizes the principles of so-called "Modern Portfolio Theory." I say "so-called" only because this theory has been around since 1967, so I am not sure it qualifies as particularly modern anymore. Based on a study by Brimson & Beebower, this theory asserts that 91% of all investment returns are related to asset allocation and portfolio diversification[9] and that only nine percent are attributable to market timing, security selection, or manager skill. If strategic management sounds a lot like passive management, it is because they have a lot in common. The difference is that we define passive management to refer to holding a specific *fund* in a portfolio, whereas we define strategic management to refer to the construction of the *portfolio* itself.

If you or your advisor should employ strategic management, it means that you will be selecting funds or managers, and in the absence of compelling rationale, you will be leaving them alone for the long-term. It does not mean that you won't periodically want to rebalance your portfolio to keep the asset allocation close to the desired one—in fact, you will absolutely want to do that to maintain the integrity of the chosen portfolio. However, it means that once you select an appropriate allocation among various asset classes (discussed in greater depth in the next chapter), you will not deviate from that allocation until and unless something changes in your *life* to justify a change of course.

On the other hand, tactical money management is a timing strategy that will have an investor moving in and out of asset classes, sectors, securities of a specific country, etc . . . on a regular basis. In that way, tactical money management means the possibility of changing direction, focus, and even risk characteristics of a portfolio constantly.

In some ways, tactical management is touted as a defensive mechanism. The idea that a tactical manager can go to cash just before a market downturn, or that, for example, the manager can get out of Greece and into Brazil *just in time*, is supposedly going to protect investor interests in avoiding big losses. While that may be true in some instances, it is equally possible to be untrue in other instances.

To me, tactical management has proliferated in the wake of the 2008 market downturn in an attempt by managers (and even some advisors) to demonstrate that they are *doing something*. In essence, the tactical managers are on the rooftops shouting that "buy-and-hold is dead." I am not so sure that is true. I am not suggesting that there is no merit to the strategy—and would not attempt to discount the value of quantitative research or the value of allowing a manager to get your assets out of harm's way when a threat is perceived. However, while tactical managers may have the ability to exit a market to protect against downside risk, they also tend to be slow to re-enter the market, thus missing potential recovery as well. In general, I see tactical management as a useful tool only as a satellite position within some portfolios, as opposed to a core investment strategy.

*   *   *   *   *

In this chapter we have discussed some of the major decisions facing investors prior to even broaching the topic of portfolio construction. Hopefully, you now have a sense of what type of investing appeals to you and what types of accounts are appropriate for you, and you are ready to start looking at asset allocation and portfolio design.

CHAPTER SEVEN

PORTFOLIO DESIGN

PRIMARY ASSET CLASSES TO CONSIDER IN YOUR MODEL ALLOCATION

Entire volumes have been written on types of savings and investment vehicles, tax implications related to saving and investing, and how to select the financial institutions that will ultimately hold your money. As it would be impossible in a few pages to do justice to this entire topic, it is my hope that this will provide a starting point for your next educational endeavor in the financial world. Please seek advice from a financial, tax, or legal professional before acting upon information in this chapter, as it is being presented in a cursory way, is very general in nature, and may not be suitable for you or your family's specific situation.

There are four primary asset classes we need to cover in this chapter, each of which has many subclasses. Those four main asset classes are as follows:

1) Cash & Cash Equivalents
2) Fixed Income Securities

3) Equities
4) Alternative Investments

This is not to suggest that all portfolios need to have access to all of these asset classes (or the various subclasses). It is to give you a broad 30,000-foot view of the investment universe to get you thinking about your portfolio on a macro-level, rather than as just a collection of holdings.

We'll start with the three traditional asset classes, and then we will talk about the "alternative" asset classes that are used for various reasons in portfolio construction.

1) Cash & Cash Equivalents

Beginning in Chapter Three, we talked about establishing an emergency fund. This is the first place where money will go when you begin to save, and with some exceptions, it may be the only place you should be putting money away until you reach the emergency or opportunity fund target.

The emergency fund will be in liquid cash or in what is frequently called a "cash equivalent" vehicle. A cash equivalent account is one that has risk similar to cash and can be converted to liquid cash basically in an instant and usually without fees or penalties.

Cash can be held in bank savings accounts, money market accounts, certificates of deposit, savings bonds, and floating rate funds (made up of ultra-short-term senior bank debt instruments). For most families, a basic savings account or money market account at a bank or credit union is absolutely fine. This is not a place to get fancy. If you are going to hold assets in the bank, make sure the funds are covered by FDIC insurance so that in the event of a bank failure, your accounts (up to a high limit—currently $250,000) are backed by the full faith and credit of the U.S. Treasury. In some brokerage firms, multiple banking institutions can be utilized in the same account to increase dramatically the FDIC insurance on cash for account holders who want to maintain very large cash positions, but as emergency funds seldom need to be larger than the single bank limit, that is not a critical issue in this context.

*   *   *   *   *

2) Fixed Income Securities

Fixed income securities can take many forms—bonds, bills, notes, commercial paper—and can be differentiated by type, by time horizon (maturity), by credit quality, by issuer, by currency, etc . . . . In other words, fixed income as a category is very broad.

Conventional wisdom suggests that bonds and other fixed income securities (to be used interchangeably throughout this section) are less volatile than stocks. In fact, the Three Factor Model that won a Nobel Prize in Economics for Professors Eugene Fama and Kenneth French included that wisdom as factor #1 of the three. Bonds are used in portfolios for two primary reasons—1) to dampen volatility in the overall portfolio and/or 2) for income purposes. In that sense, fixed income securities can be purchased for total return—meaning both capital appreciation and income potential. Most fixed income instruments pay a stated coupon rate for a stated period of time until maturity, when the face amount is returned to the investor.

Essentially, buying a bond is *loaning* money to a corporation or local, state, or federal government in exchange for interest payments. Bonds can be bought when they are issued at maturity value, or they can be bought in the open market at any time prior to maturity—possibly at a premium over maturity value or possibly at a discount to maturity value, depending on which direction interest rates have moved since the bonds were issued, investor sentiment, credit quality changes, etc . . . .

The market value of a bond tends to move in the opposite direction from trending interest rates. That is, if you own a bond paying four percent interest and current interest rates cause bonds to be issued at six percent you would expect to receive less than the maturity value for your 4% bond if you tried to sell it in the open market prior to maturity. The same is true in reverse as well. If you are getting six percent on a bond and current interest rates are at four percent, someone would be willing to pay you more than the maturity value for your bond in the open market in order to get a higher-than-market interest payment.

Some fixed income securities have specific tax advantages. For example, municipal bonds, issued by local governments, tend to provide income that is not taxed at the federal level and often at the *state* level for residents of the issuing state. Some federal agencies offer triple income tax-free bonds not taxed for income at any level. Of course, if a bond is tax-free, the interest payment will tend to be lower, so whether taxable or tax-free bonds make sense for you will depend on your income tax bracket and the prevailing interest rates at the time.

You will want to avoid owning tax-free bonds of any kind in a qualified retirement account or IRA, since those accounts offer tax deferral and you generally won't get any additional benefit from the tax-favored nature of the bonds.

Another factor in determining the volatility and income and growth potential of fixed income is the credit quality. Highly rated bonds (those rated AA and AAA, by Standard & Poors) pay the lowest interest rates because they carry the least amount of default risk (defined as the issuers' inability to continue making interest payments or to return the principal at maturity). On the other hand, so-called "junk bonds" are high yield instruments because their risk of default is much higher and therefore the interest payment and overall anticipated return must be greater to induce investors to buy them.

Think of it in the same light as two potential car buyers walking into a dealership. If you walk in with a high credit score, your risk of default is low and you'll get a much better interest rate on a car loan than if your credit score is low and you have a history of defaults. With a low credit score, you will pay a higher interest rate for the same car loan, *if* you can qualify for the loan at all!

Generally, the longer the term a bond carries, the higher the rate of interest will be on the bond. This is not always true, but it is common. That is because in order to induce investors to tie up their principal for a longer period of time, they need to be offered a higher rate of interest. It is not much different than a five-year CD at the bank paying more than a six-month CD. In addition, the longer the term that a bond has remaining until its maturity date, generally the more volatile the market price will be in the secondary bond market.

Some bonds are issued by U.S. corporations or governments, and some are issued by foreign corporations or governments. While international bonds carry additional potential risks due to currency fluctuation against the dollar or potentially less predictable political or legislative climates (subjectively to us in the U.S. anyway), they can also create a nice currency hedge and an excellent diversifier for a portfolio. As such, our firm tends to use international bonds as up to 50% of the fixed income portion of the portfolio. Some of the bonds will be from developed world countries and others will be emerging market debt, and we tend to use both in an attempt to approximate the market weightings of the total aggregate global investment universe.

When interest rates are very low, investors tend to favor short-term fixed income instruments over long-term ones. This is because you don't want to lock-in a low rate of income for a long period of time. Rational investors choose to give up some yield in the short-term to avoid giving up potentially more significant yield in the long-term.

Note that buying individual bonds and buying bond mutual funds or exchange-traded funds are not the same and they should be treated differently. In a large bond portfolio (say $500,000 or more), it may make sense to use individual bonds so that some control can be maintained in terms of credit quality, issuer and industry diversification, and length of time to maturity. You can use individual bonds to match-up up your income needs with the yield of each bond (or the portfolio as a whole). If you plan to hold bonds until they mature, you may not care as much about the market value of each bond. On the other hand, with bond funds, you are allowing a manager to allocate into a diverse portfolio, you lose the ability to match-up your income and time-horizon directly to the holdings in the fund, and at some point taking income may mean selling shares of the fund. As a result, the market price of the fund itself can become very important to you.

Whether you should be holding zero percent of your portfolio in fixed income or 100% (or more than likely somewhere in between) is beyond the scope of this book and starts to get into specific advice. However, you can utilize your financial advisor or various online resources to turn your risk tolerance profile into a suitable portfolio for your family.

*   *   *   *   *

3) Equities

When someone asks you in passing, "What did the market do today?" in the U.S., they typically mean the stock market. Oddly enough, the market index most closely followed by the news media and general public is the Dow Jones Industrial Average (DJIA)[10], which is comprised of only 30 stocks. Thus, in a world with some 15,000+ public companies, to us "the market" is only 30 of them! In fairness, the Dow is designed to be a placeholder of sorts for the overall U.S. equity markets, but there are plenty of days when the S&P 500, the Nasdaq[11], the Wilshire, the Russell, and/or other indices move in different directions than the DJIA, and on a daily basis their volatility and index movements can vary widely.

A typical mutual fund portfolio built by our firm will have upwards of 12,000 underlying securities included in it, including shares of stock in 3,000-4,000 of the public companies and some 8,000 fixed income securities. So while the DJIA's closing level every afternoon makes for interesting trivia, it does not represent the overall outcome of a typical portfolio. The only portfolio the DJIA would mirror is the portfolio that only owned those 30 stocks—no international stocks, small cap stocks, bonds or other fixed income, etc. In other words, it is interesting, but not terribly important except as it relates to the American investors' psyche.

As in the universe of fixed income securities, there are lots of different kinds of equity investments, and they can be sorted in many ways as well, but the most common ways to sort them are as follows:

- By size of company (from smallest to largest: nano-cap, micro-cap, small-cap, mid-cap, large-cap, and mega-cap)[12]
- By investment style (growth stocks vs. value stocks)[13]
- By country of domicile
- By sector or industry (technology, healthcare, financial services, etc . . .)

As believers in passive management that is not tied to an index, our firm tends to advocate for holding funds of various types that approximate the sum of the global markets in equities, as we do in fixed income. Up to 50% of our equity holdings will be in non-U.S. companies—generally split between developed nations and emerging markets.

In addition to Factor #1 suggesting that bonds and other fixed income securities are less volatile than stocks, the Fama/French 3-Factor Model identifies two other biases related to equity size and style.

Factor #2 suggests that over time, small companies will tend to outperform larger ones. This makes some sense because smaller companies have more *room* to grow. However, since small company stocks carry more risk than more stable large company stocks, it is also important to make sure we own *lots* of them for diversification purposes. We may not get rich by picking the *next* Microsoft, Google, or Apple but our portfolio also won't implode by overweighting WorldCom, Enron, or Lehman Brothers.

Factor #3 suggests that over time, value stocks will outperform growth stocks. Again, this makes some sense because, by definition, a value stock is one that is presently trading below its intrinsic value. In other words, it is *on sale*. The stock market is a funny anomaly in the human condition. It is the only place (along perhaps with the real estate markets, but more so) where people are afraid to buy something that is inexpensive. Every November, on Black Friday, when Macy's has a sale, there could be a line around the building at 4:00 in the morning, but when stocks are on sale, people instinctively think something is *wrong* with them. This isn't the damaged and defective clearance aisle; it is an opportunity to find quality companies trading at below market values.

Maintaining a bias towards small companies and value stocks is not a magic formula or a "get rich quick" plan; it is simply a methodology informing our money managers what to overweight when buying and holding for the long term. Note that there are always time frames, even recently, when one or both of these factors fails to hold true.

Before we move on from the three traditional asset classes, I'd like to share some thoughts on portfolio rebalancing. Much ado is made over the ideal time and frequency to rebalance a portfolio. Some advisors suggest annual rebalancing, some quarterly, and some as often as necessary when style-drift has occurred. Rebalancing a portfolio means selling securities that have become over-weighted and buying securities that have become under-weighted in a portfolio. In English, that means selling some of the winners and buying more of the losers in the portfolio. This is counter-intuitive, but also very important. If you do not rebalance a portfolio during a bull market, your exposure to equities may become higher than your risk tolerance would support. Likewise, if you do not rebalance a portfolio during a bear market, your exposure to equities may become lower than your risk tolerance suggests and could impair your portfolio's ability to recover from a downturn.

There are several reasons to avoid rebalancing too frequently. First, every time you rebalance, additional trading costs can impact your portfolio adversely. Secondly, in a non-qualified account, rebalancing before a full calendar year has passed can create short-term capital gains, which are taxed at the same rate as ordinary income. Lastly, rebalancing too frequently can reduce the possibility of profiting from sustained momentum amongst the so-called winners in the portfolio. Therefore, I believe that in the absence of a major event (see also: September 2008), rebalancing every 13 months or so manages costs, reduces the possibility of adverse short-term capital gains taxes (generally applied only to assets held for under a year), and allows for some momentum throughout the year as well.

Of course, there are other possible reasons to rebalance, including at the time of a large deposit or withdrawal into or out of an account, in anticipation of changing capital gain tax rates legislatively, or to harvest losses (or in some cases gains) prior to year-end for the timing of taxes due.

This section only scratched the surface on the traditional asset classes, but I hope it provided a framework to get you started and a list of things to consider when building your portfolio.

To restate this simply, the three traditional asset classes are stocks, bonds, and cash. In a bundled investment solution or a fund-of-funds which holds underlying mutual funds in a single fund wrapper, the portfolios are sometimes labeled to reflect the percentage exposure to equities versus the percentage exposure to fixed income and cash. For example, if you own a 60/40 portfolio, typically that means that you have 60% of your portfolio in stocks and 40% in bonds and cash.

*   *   *   *   *

4) Alternative Investments[14]

As the name suggests, alternative investments are those investments *not included* in the category of traditional investments above.

Alternative investments carry very different kinds of risk and return parameters than stocks, bonds, and cash, and should only be used with complete understanding of the upside and downside of doing so.

Endowments at major universities, and ultra-high net worth families ($25,000,000+) have been using alternative investments as a fairly substantial portion of their portfolios for many years. However, only in the last decade or so have these investments become readily available to retail investors.

There are six primary types of alternative investments and most investors will hold no more than two or three of them at any given time. The types are:

- Real Estate
- Managed Futures Contracts
- Hard Assets / Equipment Leasing Funds
- Hedge Funds / Funds of Hedge Funds
- Oil & Gas Partnerships
- Private Equity or Debt / Venture Capital

Each of these categories contain details which vary widely from issuer to issuer, so I strongly encourage you to talk to your advisor about them and to read the prospectuses and other legal disclosures before adding any of these assets to your portfolio.

- **Real Estate:**

For most investors, real estate investing is their first foray into the alternative investment world. This does not mean buying a townhouse, apartment building, or office building to rent and manage on your own. Unless you intend to start a real estate enterprise, including buying, selling, leasing, and managing the properties, owning just one or two rental properties is a good way to become under-diversified immediately.

Investing in real estate is typically done through a real estate investment trust (a REIT)—which can be traded on an exchange or non-traded and owned privately—or through a mutual fund or exchange-traded fund (ETF) that owns traded REITs.

To me, with the exception of a fund that tracks an index, real estate is not something to own in any significant way in a mutual fund, or even in a traded equity position. The reason is that with a mutual fund (specifically an open-ended investment company), redemption of shares must be on demand at the close of the market every day. Imagine a situation in which a large number of shareholders decide to sell at the same time. It isn't like stocks that can be sold on an open market; you're talking about buildings that can take months or longer to sell. To avoid having to sell properties in a hurry to accommodate fund redemptions that could be devastating in the real estate market, real estate funds often own liquid assets. As a result, traded real estate correlates very closely to equity indices, so it may limit diversification when more is actually being sought.

Alternatively, you can choose to own non-traded REITs, which are bought directly from sponsors and are held generally for seven to ten years with limited or no liquidity. The ideal scenario would be to receive dividends based on earnings in the trust (which can be reinvested, often at a discounted price, or can be taken in cash) and then to hold the shares until a liquidating event. That liquidating event can be the sale of the whole trust or parts of it, the sale of underlying assets in the trust, or the initial public offering or listing on an exchange that makes the trust liquid at which time we would generally explore selling the shares for the reasons described above.

Real estate trusts can be broad in nature—a core commercial real estate trust may hold office buildings, industrial warehousing space, hotels, apartment complexes, retail space, and/or other types of commercial properties. The trusts can also be sector specific—healthcare buildings, golf courses, hospitality and hotels, office buildings, etc . . .

Non-traded real estate trusts are typically commissionable vehicles, and, as such, they are held directly with sponsors, in retail brokerage accounts, or as assets excluded from asset management fees in fee-based wrap accounts.

One of the reasons that we like commercial real estate can be gleaned from the example of Enron. When Enron failed in the early 2000s, the once-raging stock became worthless and the bonds defaulted. However, they kept paying their rent to the bitter end. The landlord got paid, even when some employees didn't. That is the power of real estate—if a company doesn't pay its rent, the real estate property is collateral and can potentially be re-let or sold by the owner. As long as a company is trying to avoid bankruptcy or to exit from a bankruptcy already declared, real estate payments are often one of the last things to default because most companies would literally cease to exist without their physical space if it was mission-critical, whether that space is a store-front, a warehouse, or a manufacturing plant.

As you might expect from our conversation on equities and fixed income, we generally want to hold some of our real estate in the U.S., and some internationally, although we tend to stick to developed nations and to avoid emerging markets in this investment space due, in large part, to political uncertainty.

- **Managed Futures Contracts:**

Futures contracts are, by themselves, one of the most aggressive asset classes considered for most portfolios. That is because they are literally contracts to accept delivery or to make delivery of physical commodities—natural resources, precious metals, financial contracts, or agricultural crops for example.

They can also be "bets" on the future movement of various indices, equity markets or interest rates.

The technical reason that we would consider such an aggressive asset class for a portfolio is that the correlation coefficient is small or slightly negative for most other asset classes we hold. In plain English, that means that returns on managed futures contracts do not behave like any other asset class and therefore can create less volatility in a portfolio, even though, by itself, it is a volatile asset.

It is not uncommon to see full five percent swings in managed futures from one month to another, so it is important if you own them that you can tolerate those price movements, and that they are a small enough portion of the portfolio that a terrible quarter or year in this asset class wouldn't damage the overall portfolio returns too severely.

In 2008, managed futures were a saving grace for many portfolios, posting positive returns when nearly every other asset class was dropping precipitously. However, they have also had stretches of time like 2010-12 when they held down the overall portfolio returns with what I consider to be subpar results. As our firm does not try to time markets, we do not flit in and out of this or any asset class and we take the good with the bad. As such, we maintain this asset class in many portfolios as a small position.

Managed futures can be owned as mutual funds or as direct investments with asset managers. Most of these funds have daily or monthly liquidity, so the risk of being stuck in a long-term investment without access to capital in these positions is limited.

- ## Hard Assets / Equipment Leasing Funds:

Sometimes it is good not to be a bank. Investing in leasing funds is one such time. Leasing funds make intermediate term leases (usually four years or less) on equipment to companies to allow them to obtain and run business-necessary equipment when they cannot get bank financing directly. As the credit crisis of 2008-09 proved, it is vital to have access to capital, and when banks aren't lending, someone needs to step in and keep major companies operating.

The loan and lease agreements tend to be at very high interest rates, and the equipment or the property subject to the lease or loan agreement becomes the collateral for the lease or loan. Most importantly, because the equipment is critical to business operations, the companies need to make their lease payments or they risk being out of business. In that sense, these lease agreements are much like the real estate leases—they get paid until the bitter end or companies cease to exist.

These funds are extremely illiquid and typically run for seven to ten years. Because the investors in the fund are limited partners as opposed to stockholders, they usually receive a K-1 tax document (instead of a 1099), which means that some of the income from the program is considered non-taxable return of principal in the early years.

These funds should *only* be held in non-qualified accounts to avoid triggering unrelated business taxable income (UBTI), which can subject a qualified account to unnecessary taxes and possibly to penalties, as well.

Income expectations for these funds are targeted between eight and nine percent, but again are not guaranteed, and in the event of multiple loan or lease defaults could become worthless. Not only do you need to understand what you are buying, you also need to have complete comfort with and confidence in the firm running the lending and leasing program. Track record is important in this space, as are underlying loans and leases already in a fund if you buy it during the early to middle stage of the program.

As the loans and leases end, they can either be renewed or the equipment can be packaged and sold by the sponsor firm, with the gains (if any) divided amongst the investors. These funds are usually self-liquidating, which means that income payments made are partially return-of-capital and therefore no principal is returned at the end of the program.

- **Hedge Funds / Funds of Hedge Funds:**

Very few investment vehicles cause as much public outcry as hedge funds. That is because compared to most investment vehicles, they are loosely regulated and afforded some very favorable tax treatment, much to the chagrin of the general public.

In some ways, hedge funds are "black boxes." Some lack transparency and reporting and, as a result, their results vary wildly from time to time and from fund to fund. They are also very expensive, with fund managers making two percent per year plus up to 20% of the fund's upside in many cases.

Technically, hedge funds are not an asset class, but are an *access* class, providing access to alternative investment exposure. As the hedge can be broadly defined, each of these investment instruments is somewhat unique and carries some risks unique to the fund and its holdings.

The risk is extremely high and these investments are not appropriate for everyone; they are for savvy investors looking for additional potential upside and willing to take on the risk of complete default, as single-manager hedge funds do blow up from time-to-time.

For those reasons, you may prefer to use "funds of hedge funds," which allow access to up to 30 or 40 hedge funds within a single investment vehicle. In other words, rather than sending $100,000 to a single hedge fund manager, you can use a pooled investment and send what amounts to $2,500 to each of 40 hedge fund managers. These funds of funds give an investor the potential upside without the need for precision in terms of selecting which hedge fund will outperform the pack. It also allows investors to weather the storm if one or more of the underlying hedge funds blow up entirely.

Once again, there are no guarantees of returns, and these instruments are only for a small piece (five percent or less) of large portfolios (usually $1,000,000 or more).

Oil & Gas Partnerships:

There are very few asset classes that I simply am too uncomfortable to own or represent, and oil and gas partnerships are one of them. These partnerships aim to profit either from working interests in oil or natural gas or from exploration to try to find new sources of oil or natural gas (think Jed Clampett).

These partnerships qualify for some of the most favorable tax treatment of any investment vehicle. However, the problem I have with these partnerships isn't the income stream, the process of drilling, the politics, or any of the mechanics of the operation; the problem is the extreme liability assumed by each shareholder.

In order to be a shareholder, and to get what is a very sizable income tax deduction up-front, each investor must be willing to be a *general* partner for a period of time, prior to becoming a *limited* partner. While limited partners have liability only to the extent of their investment of capital, general partners have *unlimited liability* in the event of a lawsuit. Thus, if the fracking process for natural gas or the drilling process for oil goes wrong and creates contamination of an area impacting people or wildlife, the lawsuit that follows can name each general partner, and each one can lose *everything they own* if the suit is settled or resolved in favor of the plaintiffs in excess of the partnership's liability insurance coverage.

I looked at several of these partnerships as a financial advisor and as a possible personal investor— who wouldn't want a big tax break? However, after my personal due diligence, I couldn't get comfortable enough to own these partnership interests, which meant I wasn't comfortable enough to encourage my clients to own these partnership interests.

I perceive the upside to be significant, especially in the more speculative drilling, but the downside risk of principal loss and, more importantly, the legal risk as a general partner took this asset class completely off my personal radar. Until and unless there is a new structure to allow access to this type of investment with truly limited liability, I will continue to avoid it and to advise our firm's clients to do the same. If you elect to participate, do so with extreme caution.

- **Private Equity or Debt / Venture Capital:**

The last of the alternative investments is perhaps the most exciting, but access to some of the programs can be limited in some cases to only the wealthiest potential buyers. Private equity, private debt, and venture capital funds are designed to help start-up and privately-owned companies grow, and while the downside of starting new ventures is significant, the upside for investors who help fund growth in private companies can be huge.

The upside generally includes "deal-sweeteners" like warrants (derivative securities that provide an investor the right to purchase securities from the issuer at a specific price within a certain time frame) or an outright equity stake in the private companies, such that when one of them makes it big, the investors do extremely well.

Private equity funds are very illiquid and can require a significant contribution of capital. A minimum initial investment is often in the ballpark of $400,000. Thus, if it is an investor's intention to use private equity as a five percent alternative holding in a portfolio and the minimum contribution is $400,000, that means only an investor with a portfolio of $8,000,000 or more may be appropriate for this type of investment. That said, for the right families, these investments can create significant windfalls if the risk is properly offset by the fund managers' selection of investment opportunities.

On the other hand, private equity or private debt funds can be structured as Business Development Companies (BDCs), which provide access to this asset class with a much more modest minimum investment and simplified income tax treatment. These funds invest in small, upcoming businesses in the U.S., are regulated by the Investment Act of 1940, and get a 1099 income-tax treatment. They are more similar to REITs than to limited partnerships or other structures.

In my opinion, BDCs can offer additional diversification and portfolio upside for those investors willing to accept limited liquidity for a period of years, particularly in a flat or rising interest rate environment.

*   *   *   *   *

Please note that while an endowment is designed to be perpetual, a household is not, so only modest use of alternatives is indicated for most households. Many alternative investments are illiquid and cannot be readily sold, which means they must be used sparingly enough to avoid a situation where an investor gets into a cash crunch and can't get capital from their portfolio. In your specific situation, you will need to analyze and understand the various risks and uses for alternatives, and to make sure you have a clear understanding of what you are buying before you do so.

*   *   *   *   *

To close this section on portfolio construction, if you are just getting started with investing, you will likely be investing in some pooled investment vehicle like a mutual fund or exchange-traded fund (ETF). Both of these vehicles offer significant diversification with reasonable expenses. In other words, it would be tough to buy lots of individual stocks or bonds each month with a few hundred dollars, but in a mutual fund or ETF, a few hundred dollars a month could buy you very small positions in a very large number of different stocks, bonds, or other assets.

When investing, you always need to consider your risk tolerance, your objectives, various expenses involved, and the types of asset classes appropriate for you, and you may want to utilize a financial or tax advisor (or both) to assist in your selection and monitoring of your portfolio.

CHAPTER EIGHT

PUTTING IT ALL TOGETHER

SUMMARIZING THE STEPS TO WEALTH BUILDING AND FINANCIAL INDEPENDENCE

Let me begin this discussion by saying that it is generally much easier to *stay* wealthy, than it is to *become* wealthy. Thus, our objective here is to help families who want to begin building wealth to do so, and to plant the seeds for various action steps that can be taken at various thresholds of wealth.

Remember that for our purposes, wealth was defined by reaching a net worth such that work becomes largely optional from a financial standpoint.

In the final analysis, there are only three sources of income possible in the financial world—1) people at work, 2) money at work, and 3) charity. While you are working at a job or career, your labor is creating income for you and your family. Eventually, you need to have enough assets working for you to create income so that you can end your working years. In the absence of working assets to create income, the only other possibility is some form of handout, from an individual, organization, or government agency.

What are the steps to building wealth and what are the various thresholds whereby new opportunities exist? As I see it, the primary steps to wealth building are as follows:

1. Stay free from adverse debt.

Until and unless adverse debt can be eliminated, no level of financial independence can be achieved. This debt must be wiped off your family's balance sheet before other steps can be undertaken. This includes all credit card debt and consumer debt, all 401(k) loans, any unfavorable or variable student loans, all margin loans, and most loans against life insurance policies. It does not include debt that is leverage for real property (a mortgage or home equity line-of-credit, for example), as long as there is positive equity in the event of an immediately necessitated sale of the collateralized property.

2. Spend less than you make.

As we discussed earlier, positive cash flow is critical to making sure that you are accruing assets and avoiding debt. However large or small your income, as long as you earn more than you spend, you will have the ability to begin growing wealth. If you spend more than you earn, you will need to increase your income or decrease your expenses (or both) to have any chance to build sustainable wealth.

3. Build a risk management plan, including an emergency fund.

We have already discussed the concepts of risk management and the importance of an emergency fund for you and your family. In the absence of a comprehensive risk management plan and a suitable emergency fund, any wealth building can quickly be derailed by any number of adverse events or circumstances. Remember that a financial plan is only *ideal* if it works regardless of what happens to you. If you have loose ends in your risk management plan, get them closed before attempting to build wealth or you risk losing your progress due to unforeseen events against which you have not immunized your financial plan.

4. Pay yourself first.

In Chapter Five, I introduced you to the most important bill you need to pay each month—the one to yourself. Once you have eliminated adverse debt and created positive cash flow and a risk management plan, it is time to set up an automatic bill payment to your own savings and/or investment accounts. This will help ensure that you are building wealth.

A word about automatic bill-paying: when you decide on an amount to save or invest, I urge you to make it an automatic deduction or transfer of some kind. Whether it is from your paycheck or from your checking account, if the savings and investment deposits are automated, you can spare yourself from the psychological torture of deciding if "now is a good time to invest" or if you "want" to make a contribution in a given month. The only way this step works in your favor is to avoid the self-talk and rationalization that can be hazardous to your wealth building efforts!

5. Diversify among types of accounts.

As we addressed in Chapter Six, it is important to have both retirement (qualified) and non-retirement (non-qualified) assets in your portfolio. This is due to the various and ever-changing tax laws, and to the restrictions present on retirement accounts. When you begin to diversify your portfolio, start with different *types* of accounts, which allow you to have multiple layers of working assets. When it comes time to stop contributing and start withdrawing from the various accounts, you will find there is a great deal of flexibility when you have different "buckets of money" from which to withdraw, especially if they allow for "tax diversification" – that is the ability to decide from which accounts to withdraw in a given year based upon your income (and income tax) situation for the year.

6. Diversify among traditional asset classes.

As we discussed in Chapter Seven, for most investors, there are three primary asset classes in which to invest: equities (stocks and stock mutual funds), fixed income (bonds), and cash (and cash equivalents). The allocation to equities appropriate for you will depend on factors including your age, years to retirement, risk tolerance, and your experience and comfort as an investor. There are hundreds (if not thousands) of ways to select equities, fixed income instruments, and cash for a portfolio, and I hope Chapter Seven provided a good starting point for doing so.

Remember that the most powerful factor in determining your success in building a portfolio is in the asset allocation and diversification of the account, not in the timing or security selection.[15] It is ok to utilize several different styles of investment management, but it is more important to get the allocation right, to dollar-cost average regularly and automatically, and to manage the *behavioral* risks (often with the help of your financial advisor), which can hurt the portfolio as much as any other type of risk, if not more.

7. As appropriate, expand into alternative asset classes.

While the primary asset classes discussed above are a good starting point, as your portfolio grows, it may make sense to add alternative investments to create additional diversification. Note that these alternative investments, in and of themselves, tend to have greater risk associated with them, including liquidity risk. Thus, they are not for everyone. However, if you have built some working assets (say $100,000), it may make sense to begin introducing one or more alternative investments as a small piece of your portfolio. In general terms, alternative investments include: real estate, managed futures, commodities, precious metals, hedge funds, hard assets and equipment, natural resources (oil and natural gas, for example), private equity, private debt, and venture capital. Some of these are appropriate for a small piece of your portfolio when it reaches $100,000, while others are not appropriate for families unless they have amassed $8,000,000 or so in total working assets. As you can see, there are lots of variables and thresholds, and you will want to work with an independent financial advisor for assistance in determining which asset classes may be right for you.

8. Consider income investments as you approach retirement.

With the exception of FDIC-insured savings accounts, the word "guarantee" is one that is difficult to find in any investment vehicle, and even when it is used, it is most likely backed only by a promise from an insurance company, bank, or other financial institution. That being said, there are different types of accounts that become appropriate in some cases as individuals and couples near retirement age, which are classified as "income investments."

There are many different kinds of investments that fit that description, and they are beyond the scope of this book. However, while I firmly believe that there is rarely such a thing as a "good" or "bad" investment vehicle, there are absolutely vehicles that can be used appropriately or inappropriately for a given family situation. Used properly, they can provide additional financial security when it is needed most. You may want to explore the pros and cons of holding some of your assets in investment vehicles with fixed or stated income payments as you near and enter retirement, as they often have lifetime income benefits worth considering.

9. Maintain a current estate plan.

In Chapter Four, we included estate planning documents in the risk management area of personal financial planning. Having these documents executed properly and updated as necessary to keep them in line with your family's needs and wishes and federal and state tax laws is a critical part of the process. Building wealth that you can rely upon for your lifetime is important, but having a plan for beyond your lifetime is also a conversation worth engaging with a qualified estate planning attorney to discuss.

Our firm suggests reviewing your estate planning documents with your attorney at least every five years, or as impactful changes occur in your life—a birth or death in the family, a marriage or divorce impacting you personally or your extended family (especially if it involves one or more people you have named as responsible parties), or a geographic move. Generally, you'll want to have these documents prepared in your current state of residence, as the rules surrounding property titles and inheritance and estate tax laws vary so widely from state-to-state.

10. Hire an independent Certified Financial Planner™ practitioner and assemble your own personal "Dream Team" of advisors.

It may seem self-serving, but even objectively I cannot imagine being a busy professional and a part of a busy family and trying to stay on top of all of the planning rules, laws, and concepts on my own. I encourage you to consider the services of a financial advisor to assist you on your wealth building quest. I am asked on a regular basis how to find a planner. My first suggestion is that you ask a friend, coworker, or family member for an introduction to their planner. You can also ask your accountant, attorney, or other advisor (insurance, real estate, etc . . .) for a referral. If you are unable to get the names of one or more planners to interview, try the Planner Search feature on the website of the Financial Planning Association, or FPA. The FPA has 28,000 or so members across the United States, and their website can allow you to search for planners in your area and to find out more about their typical clientele. To access this information, go to www.fpanet.org and click on "Find a Planner."

When selecting an advisor, you will want to review his or her credentials and make sure that they reveal a background in financial planning. There are many industry-specific credentials and designations, some of which take years of study to earn and others that are mere certificates of participation. In general, look for the Certified Financial Planner™ or (CFP®) designation, as it is considered the gold standard for the financial planning industry. To earn a CFP® designation, a candidate must pass six (6) courses and a two-day, 10-hour board exam. Additionally the candidate must have at least three (3) years of experience in the field, and most importantly, must maintain objectivity and act as a fiduciary while keeping the client's best interests in mind.

Note that some advisors work for various financial institutions as captive agents or employees, which can limit the range of products or services available to their clients. Other advisors are independent and have an open range of products and services available to their clients manufactured by multiple financial institutions. At the end of the day, you wouldn't see a doctor without an M.D., so in my opinion, it is important to know if an advisor is a CFP® or not, and also to whom the advisor is primarily responsible—their employer or their clients.

Before choosing to work with an advisor or firm, you may want to conduct a professional background check on them. You may also want to see if they have a history of complaints against them or if they have been involved in a personal bankruptcy or have had legal actions taken against them.

To research a potential advisor, you can verify that your advisor is a CFP Practitioner by going to the CFP Board's website at www.cfp.net. You can also check disciplinary history by using the Financial Industry Regulatory Authority's Broker-Check, which is available online at www.finra.org.

You generally will want to fall within the scope of a typical client for a firm. Unless you have been referred to a specific financial advisor by a trusted friend or advisor, I encourage you to interview several planners before making a decision. We discussed some of the questions you might want to ask a prospective financial advisor in Chapter Two.

In Chapter Six, we talked about some of the risks inherent in investing, and about the risk tolerance questionnaire completed by investors during the data gathering process. The problem is that some firms will stop with the risk tolerance questionnaire and will implement investment portfolios based on the questionnaire responses alone. This is called meeting the "suitability standard." The suitability standard is one to which most stock brokers, bank employees, and insurance agents are held. It says that all investment recommendations must be *suitable* for a particular client *at the time they are recommended.*

This standard is not nearly high enough in my mind, but the battles in Congress on the issue are facing stiff lobbying efforts by brokerage firms, insurance companies, and banks who want their employees to be able to sell their proprietary products when they are suitable, even if they may not be the *best* solution for a client. While I understand the business rationale for this stance, if I were a client of these firms, I would always wonder if my *best interests* were being served or if I was simply getting a *suitable* product off the shelf.

The higher standard in the financial advisory profession is the "fiduciary standard." This is the standard to which Certified Financial Planner™ Practitioners are held. The fiduciary standard forces planners to put themselves in a client's shoes, and to render advice that is in the *best interests* of the client at all times. Taken one step further, the fiduciary standard ensures that I render planning advice to a client the same way I would to my own family. It doesn't mean that my family owns *everything* that a client does in his or her portfolio. It does mean, however, that if a client situation were to mirror my family's situation, our portfolios would look very similar.

*   *   *   *   *

Selecting a financial advisor is only the first step in assembling your "dream team." You will also need the services of one or more of the following professionals (if your CFP® does not perform their functions in-house):

- An attorney (estate planning, business planning, family planning) licensed in your home state
- An accountant or tax-preparer (ideally a CPA)
- A real estate agent who knows your area
- A mortgage banker or broker
- A personal banker or credit union representative
- A property and casualty insurance agent
- A life and health insurance agent
- Your human resources liaison at work

Just like in your process for choosing a CFP®, ask for referrals from other professionals or people you trust, and consider interviewing a few before making your ultimate selection. Ideally, you want all of these professionals to know what the others are doing and to work together for your benefit. Coordination of all of your planning helps avoid mistakes and may make your desired outcome more attainable.

WHAT TO DO <u>NOW</u>

I hope that you have found the time you invested in reading this book to be worthwhile and that you picked up a few strategies that will be helpful to you and your family at whatever stage of wealth building describes your situation.

If you have adverse debt, start by chipping away at it strategically. Once you are free of adverse debt, use the cash management strategies in this book, along with the risk management strategies, to take the next steps. If you have achieved positive cash flow and learned to live on 85% or so of your income, and you've built a moat around your castle with a solid risk management plan, you're ready for wealth building.

There will be setbacks along the way—that's life. But, if you can chart a path and adjust your course as necessary when life throws a detour your way, you'll be reaching your goals before you know it.

I hope you now feel empowered and armed with some of the tools you need to help you reach financial success—as *you* define it. If you decide you use a financial advisor, remember that financial planning is like medicine—you wouldn't expect to get a diagnosis without being thoroughly examined by a doctor, so take your time in finding the right advisor and invest in a comprehensive planning engagement.

I welcome your feedback on the book, and if you have a personal success story to share as a result of reading it, I'd love to hear it.

I wish you continued success in your financial future.

AUTHOR'S ACKNOWLEDGEMENTS

I would like to express special thanks to Brent Weiss, Michelle Roberts, and the entire team at Brotman Financial Group, who make sure the office runs smoothly in my absence while I am off writing books.

Thanks also to the book reviewers who read early drafts and provided the feedback needed to make this final product a reality: Michael Barnett, Vera Brown, Larry DeNoia, Lisa D'Orsaneo, David Edwin, Millard Firebaugh, Scott Oehrle, Martin and Stacey Schwartzberg, Sharon Seal, Neil Sweren, Emily Tanczyn, and Lori Villegas.

Very special thanks also go to Steven Hawtof for his assistance in structuring the publishing contract and to Liz Rivera of NFP Securities, Inc. for spending hours reading countless revisions and providing compliance support.

Most importantly, thanks to my girls—my wife, Meredith, and my daughter, Brooke, for understanding the many days I spent researching, writing, and editing to make this book happen.

Eric

APPENDIX A:

SAMPLE FINANCIAL PLANNING
QUESTIONNAIRE
PAGE 1

Home & Personal Information

Last Name _____

Home Address   Second Residence

_____   _____

_____   _____

Year of Purchase _____   Year of Purchase _____

Phone _____   Home Email _____
                                           ○ Checked Regularly   ○ Not Checked Regularly
Home Fax _____

Financial Objectives:

Primary financial concerns: _____

_____

_____

Primary financial objectives and/or aspirations: _____

_____

_____

Non-financial concerns, objectives and/or aspirations: _____

_____

_____

Advisors & Contacts

Accountant _____		Estate Attorney _____	
Firm Name _____		Firm Name _____	
Insurance Agent _____		Personal Attorney _____	
Firm Name _____		Firm Name _____	
Mortgage Broker _____		Corporate Attorney _____	
Firm Name _____		Firm Name _____	

Who referred you to us?

_____

APPENDIX A:

SAMPLE FINANCIAL PLANNING QUESTIONNAIRE PAGE 2

Client

Name _____ D/O/B _____ SS# _____

State of Birth _____ Drivers License # _____

DL State _____ DL Issue Date _____ DL Expiration Date _____

Occupation _____ Job Title _____

Employer _____ Date of Hire _____

Address _____

Office Phone _____ Office Email _____

Office Fax _____ Cell Phone _____

Education

High School _____ Graduate School _____

College _____

Compensation

Annual Base W2 Salary _____ Pay Periods Per Year _____

Bonus/Commission _____ Frequency/When Paid? _____

Self Employment Income _____

Other Compensation _____

Do you own employee stock options? ○ Yes ○ No   Are you being granted additional options regularly? ○ Yes ○ No

Father	**Mother**
Name _____	Name _____
Date of Birth _____	Date of Birth _____
State of Residence _____ ○ Deceased	State of Residence _____ ○ Deceased
Current will and POA? ○ Yes ○ No ○ Uncertain	Current will and POA? ○ Yes ○ No ○ Uncertain
Long-term care insurance? ○ Yes ○ No ○ Uncertain	Long-term care insurance? ○ Yes ○ No ○ Uncertain
Estimated net worth:	Estimated net worth:
○ < $300k ○ $300k-$1 million ○ > $1 million	○ < $300k ○ $300k-$1 million ○ > $1 million

2

APPENDIX A:

SAMPLE FINANCIAL PLANNING QUESTIONNAIRE PAGE 3

Spouse

Name _____ D/O/B _____ SS# _____

State of Birth _____ Drivers License # _____

DL State _____ DL Issue Date _____ DL Expiration Date _____

Occupation _____ Job Title _____

Employer _____ Date of Hire _____

Address _____

Office Phone _____ Office Email _____

Office Fax _____ Cell Phone _____

Education

High School _____ Graduate School _____

College _____

Compensation

Annual Base W2 Salary _____ Pay Periods Per Year _____

Bonus/Commission _____ Frequency/When Paid? _____

Self Employment Income _____

Other Compensation _____

Do you own employee stock options? ○ Yes ○ No   Are you being granted additional options regularly? ○ Yes ○ No

Father	Mother
Name _____	Name _____
Date of Birth _____	Date of Birth _____
State of Residence _____ ○ Deceased	State of Residence _____ ○ Deceased
Current will and POA? ○ Yes ○ No ○ Uncertain	Current will and POA? ○ Yes ○ No ○ Uncertain
Long-term care insurance? ○ Yes ○ No ○ Uncertain	Long-term care insurance? ○ Yes ○ No ○ Uncertain
Estimated net worth:	Estimated net worth:
○ < $300k ○ $300k-$1 million ○ > $1 million	○ < $300k ○ $300k-$1 million ○ > $1 million

3

APPENDIX A:

SAMPLE FINANCIAL PLANNING QUESTIONNAIRE PAGE 4

First Child

Name _____ D/O/B _____ SS # _____

Child of: ○ Current marriage ○ Husband ○ Wife

Dependent Child

School _____ Grade _____

College Expectations: ○ Private ○ Public/State ○ None ○ Scholarships Possible ○ Financial Aid Anticipated

College Funding Expectations: Source of Funds

○ Fully fund undergraduate tuition _____

○ Partially fund undergraduate tuition _____

○ Student loans _____

Independent Child

Occupation _____ State of Residence _____

Spouse _____

Children & Ages _____

Would you feel comfortable re-titling assets into this child's name? ○ Yes ○ No

Would you feel comfortable with this child being named a responsible
party in your estate plan (i.e. trustee, executor or power of attorney?) ○ Yes ○ No

Special needs, concerns or considerations:

Second Child

Name _____ D/O/B _____ SS # _____

Child of: ○ Current marriage ○ Husband ○ Wife

Dependent Child

School _____ Grade _____

College Expectations: ○ Private ○ Public/State ○ None ○ Scholarships Possible ○ Financial Aid Anticipated

College Funding Expectations: Source of Funds

○ Fully fund undergraduate tuition _____

○ Partially fund undergraduate tuition _____

○ Student loans _____

Independent Child

Occupation _____ State of Residence _____

Spouse _____

Children & Ages _____

Would you feel comfortable re-titling assets into this child's name? ○ Yes ○ No

Would you feel comfortable with this child being named a responsible
party in your estate plan (i.e. trustee, executor or power of attorney?) ○ Yes ○ No

Special needs, concerns or considerations:

4

171

APPENDIX A:

SAMPLE FINANCIAL PLANNING QUESTIONNAIRE PAGE 5

Third Child

Name _____ D/O/B _____ SS # _____

Child of: ○ Current marriage   ○ Husband   ○ Wife

Dependent Child

School _____ Grade _____

College Expectations: ○ Private   ○ Public/State   ○ None ○ Scholarships Possible ○ Financial Aid Anticipated

College Funding Expectations: Source of Funds

○ Fully fund undergraduate tuition   _____

○ Partially fund undergraduate tuition   _____

○ Student loans   _____

Independent Child

Occupation _____ State of Residence _____

Spouse _____

Children & Ages _____

Would you feel comfortable re-titling assets into this child's name?   ○ Yes   ○ No

Would you feel comfortable with this child being named a responsible
party in your estate plan (i.e. trustee, executor or power of attorney?)   ○ Yes   ○ No

Special needs, concerns or considerations:

_____

_____

Other Financial Dependent

Name _____ D/O/B _____ SS # _____

Relationship _____

Nature of Financial Dependency:

_____

_____

_____

Are you the primary caregiver?   ○ Yes   ○ No   If not, who is? _____

Are you the primary financial provider?   ○ Yes   ○ No   If not, who is? _____

Have any assets been transferred to you?   ○ Yes   ○ No   What amount? _____

Other relevant details:

_____

_____

5

172

APPENDIX A:

SAMPLE FINANCIAL PLANNING QUESTIONNAIRE PAGE 6

Savings & Investments

Bank and Savings Assets

	Institution	Balance	Monthly Additions	Name(s) on Account
Checking		$	$ /mo	
Checking		$	$ /mo	
Savings		$	$ /mo	
Savings		$	$ /mo	
Money Market		$	$ /mo	
Money Market		$	$ /mo	
CD		$	$ /mo	
CD		$	$ /mo	
Savings Bonds		$	$ /mo	
Savings Bonds		$	$ /mo	

Non-Retirement Investment Assets

	Institution	Balance	Monthly Additions	Name(s) on Account
Brokerage Account		$	$ /mo	
Brokerage Account		$	$ /mo	
Brokerage Account		$	$ /mo	
Mutual Fund		$	$ /mo	
Mutual Fund		$	$ /mo	
Mutual Fund		$	$ /mo	
Stock / Bond		$	$ /mo	
Stock / Bond		$	$ /mo	
Stock / Bond		$	$ /mo	
Tax Deferred Annuity		$	$ /mo	
Tax Deferred Annuity		$	$ /mo	
Tax Deferred Annuity		$	$ /mo	
Partnership		$	$ /mo	
Partnership		$	$ /mo	
529 College Savings		$	$ /mo	
529 College Savings		$	$ /mo	

APPENDIX A:

SAMPLE FINANCIAL PLANNING
QUESTIONNAIRE
PAGE 7

Retirement Assets

Personal Retirement Accounts

	Institution	Balance	Monthly Additions	Name on Account
IRA		$	$ /mo	
IRA		$	$ /mo	
IRA		$	$ /mo	
IRA		$	$ /mo	
Roth IRA		$	$ /mo	
Roth IRA		$	$ /mo	
SEP / SIMPLE		$	$ /mo	
SEP / SIMPLE		$	$ /mo	
Inherited IRA		$	$ /mo	
Inherited IRA		$	$ /mo	

Employer-Sponsored Plans

	Balance	% of Salary Contributions	Annual Employee Contributions	Annual Employer Match/Deposit	Name on Account
401(k) / 403(b)	$	%	$	$	
401(k) / 403(b)	$	%	$	$	
401(k) / 403(b)	$	%	$	$	
Pension/Profit Sharing	$	%	$	$	
Pension/Profit Sharing	$	%	$	$	
Pension/Profit Sharing	$	%	$	$	
Deferred Compensation	$	%	$	$	
Deferred Compensation	$	%	$	$	
ESOP	$	%	$	$	
Employer Stock Purchase Plan	$	%	$	$	

	Vested Benefits if Employment Terminated	Benefits at 65 if Employment Continues	Name on Account
Defined Benefit Pension	$ /mo	$ /mo	
Defined Benefit Pension	$ /mo	$ /mo	

	Projected Benefits at age 62	Projected Benefits at Normal Retirement	
Social Security	$ /mo	$ /mo	Client
Social Security	$ /mo	$ /mo	Spouse

7

174

APPENDIX A:

SAMPLE FINANCIAL PLANNING QUESTIONNAIRE PAGE 8

Real Assets

Real Estate

	Estimated Market Value	Purchase Price	Capital Improvements	Years Owned	Owner
Primary Residence					
Second Residence, Land					
Rental Property					
Rental Property					
Commercial Rental Prop.					
Commercial Rental Prop.					

Personal Assets

	Estimated Market Value		Year, Make & Model
Jewelry		Automobile #1	
Artwork		Automobile #2	
Collectibles		Auto #3, Boat, RV	

Business Ownership

Name	Business Form	% Owned	Estimated Market Value
	○Corp ○S-Corp ○LLC ○Sole Prop		
	○Corp ○S-Corp ○LLC ○Sole Prop		
	○Corp ○S-Corp ○LLC ○Sole Prop		

Trust Assets

Name	Type of Trust	Annual Income	Estimated Market Value

8

APPENDIX A:

SAMPLE FINANCIAL PLANNING QUESTIONNAIRE PAGE 9

Liabilities

	Loan Type Fixed/Adjustable	Balance	Monthly Payment	Interest Rate	Months Remaining
Mortgage (Residence)		$	$ /mo	%	
2nd Mortgage (Residence)		$	$ /mo	%	
Home Equity Line/Loan		$	$ /mo	%	
Mortgage (2nd Residence)		$	$ /mo	%	
Auto Loan / Lease		$	$ /mo	%	
Auto Loan / Lease		$	$ /mo	%	
Auto Loan / Lease		$	$ /mo	%	
Student Loan		$	$ /mo	%	
Student Loan		$	$ /mo	%	
Personal Line of Credit		$	$ /mo	%	
Credit Card		$	$ /mo	%	
Credit Card		$	$ /mo	%	
Investment Margin Loan		$	$ /mo	%	
Life Insurance Policy Loan		$	$ /mo	%	
Life Insurance Policy Loan		$	$ /mo	%	

Estate Planning

Type of Wills: ○ Simple Will   ○ By-Pass Will (Credit Shelter Trusts)   ○ Disclaimer Will

Do you have wills executed in your state of residence?   ○ Yes   ○ No   How recent? _____ /yrs

Do you have durable powers-of-attorney?   ○ Yes   ○ No   How recent? _____ /yrs

Do you have an advanced medical directive (living will)?   ○ Yes   ○ No   How recent? _____ /yrs

Do you have an irrevocable life insurance trust?   ○ Yes   ○ No

Are you making annual gifts? $ _____ /yr   Have you ever paid a gift tax?   ○ Yes   ○ No

Are you receiving annual gifts? $ _____ /yr   Have you used any of your unified credit?   ○ Yes   ○ No

9

APPENDIX A:

SAMPLE FINANCIAL PLANNING QUESTIONNAIRE PAGE 10

Risk Management

Property & Casualty Insurance

	Insurance Company	Property Limit	Liability Limit	Deductible(s)
Auto Insurance		$	$	$
Homeowners Insurance		$	$	$
Umbrella (excess liability)		$	$	$
Worker's Compensation*		$	$	$

*For domestic employees

Disability & Medical Insurance

	Insurance Company	Monthly Benefit or % of Salary Replaced	Benefit Period (Years or To Age...)	Annual Premium	Insured (Client/Spouse)
Private Disability Insurance				$	
Private Disability Insurance				$	
Employer Group LTD				$	
Employer Group LTD				$	
Health Insurance	○ Individual	○ Through Client's Employer		○ Through Spouse's Employer	

Long-Term Care Insurance

	Insurance Company	Daily Benefit	Benefit Period	Home Care Covered?	Annual Premium	Insured (Client/Spouse)
Private Insurance		$			$	
Private Insurance		$			$	
Employer Group LTC		$			$	
Employer Group LTC		$			$	

Life Insurance

	Insurance Company	Coverage Amount	Policy Type	Annual Premium	Insured (Client/Spouse)
Life Insurance		$		$	
Life Insurance		$		$	
Life Insurance		$		$	
Life Insurance		$		$	
Employer Group Life		$		$	
Employer Group Life		$		$	

10

177

APPENDIX A:

SAMPLE FINANCIAL PLANNING QUESTIONNAIRE PAGE 11

Additional Information

Desired Monthly Savings,
In Addition to Current Amounts

Minimum	$	/mo.
Realistic Goal	$	/mo.
Ideal Goal	$	/mo.

Planned Retirement Age

	Client	Spouse
Maximum		
Realistic Goal		
Ideal Goal		

Anticipated Extraordinary Expenses

Expense:	Anticipated Amount $	When	
Expense:	Anticipated Amount $	When	
Expense:	Anticipated Amount $	When	

Anticipated Extraordinary Windfalls

Windfall:	Anticipated Amount $	When	
Windfall:	Anticipated Amount $	When	
Windfall:	Anticipated Amount $	When	

Significant Recurring Expenses / Income

	Annual Amount	Anticipated End Date		Annual Amount	Anticipated End Date
Alimony	$ /yr		Child Care	$ /yr	
Child Support	$ /yr		Tuition	$ /yr	
Other	$ /yr		Other	$ /yr	

Anticipated Family, Career, Residence Changes:

_____
_____
_____

Other Relevant Information *(military background, health issues, etc.)*:

_____
_____
_____

11

178

APPENDIX A:

SAMPLE FINANCIAL PLANNING QUESTIONNAIRE PAGE 12

Risk Tolerance Questionnaire

The information provided in this questionnaire is not intended to be investment advice and does not constitute a recommendation to buy or sell securities.

1) **This graph shows the potential range of gains or losses of a $100,000 investment in each of seven hypothetical portfolios at the end of a 1-year period. The number to the right of each bar shows the best potential gain for that portfolio, while the number to the left of each bar shows the worst potential loss. Given that this is the only information that you have on these seven hypothetical portfolios, which one would you choose to invest in?**

- ○ Portfolio A
- ○ Portfolio B
- ○ Portfolio C
- ○ Portfolio D
- ○ Portfolio E
- ○ Portfolio F
- ○ Portfolio G

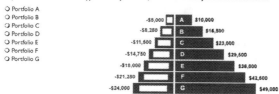

-$5,000	**A**	$10,000
-$8,250	**B**	$16,500
-$11,500	**C**	$23,000
-$14,750	**D**	$29,500
-$18,000	**E**	$36,000
-$21,250	**F**	$42,500
-$24,000	**G**	$49,000

2) **Once again, assume you have a substantial portion of your investment portfolio in stocks. If the stock market were to gradually decline at an average of 2 percent per month, eventually losing 22% of its value over a year, which of the following would you do?**

- ○ Invest more now because stocks are selling for approximately 22% less than they were 12 months ago. You believe that the stocks will regain their value or possibly appreciate even higher over the long-term.
- ○ Sell the stocks in your portfolio and realize the 22% loss. You wish to avoid the risk of further loss.
- ○ Sell half of the stocks in your portfolio. You are not willing to leave all of your investment at risk for further loss.
- ○ Do nothing. You are comfortable waiting for the stocks to regain their previous value or to increase in value.

3) **Aggressive investments have historically provided higher returns while exhibiting greater short-term price fluctuations and potential for loss. How do you feel about fluctuations in the value of your portfolio?**

- ○ You want to minimize the possibility of loss in the value of your portfolio. You understand that you are sacrificing higher long-term returns by holding investments that reduce the potential for short-term loss and price fluctuation.
- ○ You can tolerate moderate losses in order to achieve potentially favorable returns.
- ○ You can tolerate the risk of large losses in your portfolio in order to increase the potential of achieving high returns.

4) **What is the investment time horizon on these investable assets?**

- ○ Less than 3 years
- ○ 3 - 5 years
- ○ 6 - 9 years
- ○ 10+ years

5) **What is your current annual household income?**

6) **What is your approximate net worth?**

7) **What is the approximate value of your liquid assets?**

8) **What are your income needs from investable assets?**

- ○ None
- ○ $10,000 Per Year
- ○ $20,000 Per Year
- ○ $30,000 Per Year
- ○ $40,000 Per Year
- ○ $50,000 Per Year
- ○ $60,000 Per Year
- ○ $70,000 Per Year
- ○ $80,000 Per Year
- ○ $90,000 Per Year
- ○ $100,000 Per Year
- ○ More than $100,000 Per Year

APPENDIX A:

SAMPLE FINANCIAL PLANNING QUESTIONNAIRE PAGE 13

9) What is your state tax bracket?

- ○ 0%
- ○ 1%
- ○ 2%
- ○ 3%
- ○ 4%
- ○ 5%
- ○ 6%
- ○ 7%
- ○ 8%
- ⊗ 9%
- ⊗ 10%
- ⊗ Over 10 %

10) What is your federal tax bracket?

- ○ 10 %
- ○ 15 %
- ○ 25 %
- ○ 28 %
- ○ 33 %
- ○ 35 %

11) What is your investment goal or intended use of the assets?

- ○ Retirement
- ○ Education Funding
- ○ Charitable Giving
- ○ Estate Appreciation
- ○ Gifting
- ○ Other

13

APPENDIX B:

SAMPLE PERSONAL FINANCIAL PLANNING DOCUMENT CHECKLIST

Document Checklist

Please provide originals or copies of all documents appropriate to your situation, as well as any others that may be relevant. All originals will be returned during the planning process.

Legal Documents
- ○ Copy of valid drivers' license or passport
- ○ Wills
- ○ Financial Powers of Attorney
- ○ Living Wills
- ○ Advanced health care directives
- ○ Trust agreements
- ○ Pre- or post-nuptial agreements
- ○ Terms of divorce/legal separation

Taxes
- ○ Last 2 years' personal tax returns (Federal, State, W-2s, and all schedules)
- ○ Social Security benefit estimate(s)

Banking
- ○ Checking account statement(s)
- ○ Savings/money market statement(s)
- ○ CD statement(s)
- ○ Debt/loan details

Investments
- ○ Brokerage account statement(s)
- ○ Mutual fund account statement(s)
- ○ IRA/Roth IRA account statement(s)
- ○ Stock dividend reinvestment plan(s)
- ○ Partnership/private investment document
- ○ Cost basis for all existing investments

Retirement Plan
- ○ 401(k)/403(b) statement(s)
- ○ Summary plan description
- ○ Deferred compensation agreement(s)
- ○ Pension/profit-sharing statement(s)
- ○ Proof of beneficiary designations for all account(s)

Real Estate & Personal Property
- ○ Mortgage statement/document(s)
- ○ Home equity loan/line-of-credit statement(s)
- ○ Investment property cash flow statement(s)
- ○ Deed(s) for real property
- ○ Proof of title for automobile(s)

Insurance
- ○ Auto & homeowners declaration pages
- ○ Personal liability umbrella declaration pages
- ○ Disability policies
- ○ Life insurance policies and annual statements
- ○ Proof of beneficiary designations for all policies

Employee Benefits
- ○ Recent pay stubs
- ○ Employee benefit handbook
- ○ Annual benefit summary
- ○ Employee stock option plan documents
- ○ Employee stock option grant summary
- ○ Proof of beneficiary designations for all company plans

Other
- ○ _____
- ○ _____
- ○ _____
- ○ _____
- ○ _____
- ○ _____

Endnotes

[1]   Bank certificates of deposit are FDIC insured up to applicable limits and offer a fixed rate of return.

[2]   Policy benefits may be reduced by any policy loans, withdrawals, terminal illness benefit, or long-term care benefits paid under the policy. Death Proceeds and Return of Premium Benefit will be reduced when long-term care benefits are taken. Values assume no prior distributions of any kind taken. Certain benefits may not be available until a specific age is attained. An elimination period may apply before long-term care benefits are available. See your policy for details.

[3]   Policy benefits may be reduced by any policy loans, withdrawals, terminal illness benefit, or long-term care benefits paid under the policy. Death Proceeds and Return of Premium Benefit will be reduced when long-term care benefits are taken. Certain benefits may not be available until a specific age is attained. An elimination period may apply before long-term care benefits are available. See your policy for details. The monthly amount reimbursed is the cost of covered long-term care expenses actually incurred, which may be less than the Monthly Maximum Benefit. The Monthly Maximum Benefit may be pro-rated based on the actual number of days that the insured is chronically ill or confined to a facility. Long-term care insurance benefits may be subject to limitations, waiting periods, and other restrictions.

[4]   Variable life insurance products, which are subject to market risk including possible loss of principal, allow the contract holder to choose

an appropriate amount of life insurance protection that has an additional cost associated with it. Care should be taken to ensure these strategies and products are suitable for your long-term life insurance needs. You should weigh your objectives, time horizon, and risk tolerance as well as any associated costs before investing. Also, be aware that market volatility can lead to the possibility of the need for additional premium in your policy. Variable life insurance has fees and charges associated with it that include costs of insurance that vary with such characteristics of the insured as gender, health and age, underlying fund charges and expenses, and additional charges for riders that customize a policy to fit your individual needs.

The sub-accounts in variable insurance products fluctuate with market conditions and when surrendered the principal may be worth more or less than the original amount invested.

All guarantees are subject to the claims-paying ability of the issuing insurance company. Guarantees do not apply to the investment performance of any variable accounts, which are subject to market risk.

[5]   Trusts should be drafted by an attorney familiar with such matters in order to take into account income, gift, and estate tax laws (including generation-skipping transfer tax). Failure to do so could result in adverse tax treatment of trust proceeds.

[6]   All guarantees are based on the financial strength and claims paying ability of the issuing insurance company, who is solely responsible for all obligations under its policies.

[7]   Dollar-cost averaging does not assure a profit and does not protect against a loss in declining markets. This strategy involves continuous investing; you should consider your financial ability to continue purchases no matter how prices fluctuate.

8   **S&P 500 Index**—The S&P 500 Index is an unmanaged group of securities considered to be representative of the stock market in general. You cannot directly invest in the index.

9   Asset allocation does not protect against loss of principal due to market fluctuations. It is a method used to help manage investment risk.

10 **Dow Jones Industrial Average**—The Dow Jones Industrial Average is a popular indicator of the stock market based on the average closing prices of 30 active U.S. stocks representative of the overall economy. You cannot invest directly into the index.

11 NASDAQ Composite Index measures all NASDAQ domestic and international based common stocks listed on The NASDAQ Stock Market. Today the NASDAQ Composite includes approximately 5,000 stocks, more than most other stock market indices. Because it is so broad-based, the Composite is one of the most widely followed and quoted major market indices.

12 The terms **nano-cap**, **micro-cap**, **small-cap**, **mid-cap**, **large-cap**, and **mega-cap** refer to the stock of public companies in the U.S. which have a market capitalization as follows:

- Nano-cap: Below $50 million
- Micro-cap: Below $250 million
- Small-cap: $250 million–$2 billion
- Mid-cap: $2 billion–$10 billion
- Large-cap: Over $10 billion
- Mega-cap: Over $200 billion

13 A **growth stock** is a stock of a company that generates substantial and sustainable positive cash flow and whose revenues and earnings are expected to increase at a faster rate than the average company within

the same industry. Growth stocks usually pay smaller dividends, as the company typically reinvests retained earnings in capital projects.

A **value stock** is a stock of a company that appears to be underpriced by some form of fundamental analysis. Value stocks typically trade at a discount to book value, or they have a high dividend yield, a low price-to-earnings multiple, and/or a low price-to-book ratio.

[14]   Alternative investments, including hedge funds, real estate, and managed futures, involve a high degree of risk, often engage in leveraging and other speculative investment practices that may increase the risk of investment loss, can be highly illiquid, are not required to provide periodic pricing or valuation to investors, may involves complex tax structures and delays in distributing important tax information, are not subject to the same regulatory requirements as mutual funds, often charge high fees which may offset any trading profits, and in many cases the underlying investments are not transparent and are known only to the investment manager. The performance of alternative investments, including hedge funds and managed futures, can be volatile. An investor could lose all or a substantial amount of his or her investment. These types of investments may not be suitable for all investors. Please consult with a financial or legal professional before investing in alternative investments.

[15]   Asset allocation does not protect against loss of principal due to market fluctuations. It is a method used to help manage investment risk.